Quechua

lonely planet

phrasebooks
and
Serafin M. Coronel-Molina

Quechua phrasebook
3rd edition – July 2008

Published by
Lonely Planet Publications Pty Ltd ABN 36 005 607 983
90 Maribyrnong St, Footscray, Victoria 3011, Australia

Lonely Planet Offices
Australia Locked Bag 1, Footscray, Victoria 3011
USA 150 Linden St, Oakland CA 94607
UK 2nd Floor, 186 City Rd, London EC1V 2NT

Cover illustration
Weightless – above the world by Michael Ruff

ISBN 978 1 74059 770 8

text © Lonely Planet Publications Pty Ltd 2008
cover illustration © Lonely Planet Publications Pty Ltd 2008

  10 9 8 7 6 5 4 3 2

Printed through The Bookmaker International Ltd.
Printed in China

acknowledgments

about the author

Serafín M. Coronel-Molina is a native speaker of Quechua from the Peruvian highlands with experience in indigenous language policy and planning, and second language acquisition. He has taught Spanish and Quechua at different times in various institutions in Peru, Mexico and the United States, and taught both languages at the University of Michigan for two years with a joint appointment in the Department of Romance Languages and Literatures, and the Latin American and Caribbean Studies Program. He has a PhD in Educational Linguistics from the University of Pennsylvania in Philadelphia (USA). He has published scholarly articles and presented papers both nationally and internationally relating to indigenous language policy/planning in the Andean region, and Quechua sociolinguistics, including one article written entirely in Quechua about Quechua language planning, and published in the journal Amerindia: Revue d'Ethnolinguistique Amérindienne (vol. 24). The Sustainable Travel section was created by Ozwaldo Munoz and Quentin Frayne.

from the author

No book comes into being without the help and support of many people, and this one is no exception. Thus I would like to gratefully acknowledge the patience and understanding of my wife, Linda Grabner-Coronel, and my daughter Flor de María, when I was so single-mindedly concentrating on the writing of this phrasebook. Even more, I owe my wife a large debt of gratitude for going so far as to stay up late with me many a night to help me proofread the text and keep details consistent throughout the book. I couldn't have done it without her eagle eyes. Annelies Mertens, my editor, is another person whose sharp eyes, linguistic knowledge and editorial skill helped polish the book into publishable form, and I thank her for her patience with my idiosyncratic working style. Finally, to my friend and native Quechua speaker Juan Arroyo, I offer my thanks for a helpful telephone conversation in and about Quechua, when he helped me to judge the comprehensibility of a few phrases I had struggled with. All of these people have contributed to making this

phrasebook the useful tool it is. Grateful acknowledgment is made to Rodolfo Cerrón-Palomino/Lingüística Aymara, Lima, Peru: Centro de Estudios Regionales Andinos 'Bartolomé de Las Casas' for use of data from their Quechua language map © 2000.

from the publisher

And the *Quechua phrasebook* relay is off ... first out of the gates is editor Annelies Mertens in fine style then senior editors Karin Vidstrup Monk and Karina Coates, and assisting editors Sophie Putman, Meg Worby, Sally Steward, Emma Koch, Branislava Vladisavljevic and Laura Crawford. But what's this? Coming up on the inside to oversee production are publishing managers Jim Jenkin and Ben Handicott ... neck and neck with star designer Patrick Marris, a real favourite in layout circles ... he's trained the promising yearling designer Yvonne Bischofberger, backed up by freelancer Jo Adams ... designer Yuki Kamimura's coming in from the outside to knock off Grammar but it's an upset folks, Grammar's winning! Beautiful form here from cover illustrator Michael Ruff and illustrator Rosie Silva-Guevara ... senior designer Fabrice Rocher's scheduled to come in on time and cartographers Natasha Velleley and Wayne Murphy are handling the course as if they drew the map themselves. A late entry here in layout designer David Kemp – a good finisher. What a magnificent result folks and a great end to the season!

CONTENTS

6   Contents

quechua

PRESENT-DAY QUECHUA-
SPEAKING REGIONS
Northern Quechua
Central Quechua
Southern Quechua

INTRODUCTION

Travelling in the Andes will be much more enjoyable and worthwhile if you can speak some Quechua, the language of the Incas, also known as *runasimi*, roo·nah·*see*·mee.

Despite the official status of Spanish, which was brought to Latin America by the conquistadors, you'll find that Quechua is spoken in six South American countries: Peru, Bolivia, Ecuador, Colombia, Argentina and Chile. Most Quechua speakers are found in the Andes, although some live in the jungle or on the coast.

Quechua is actually a family of languages that has been spoken by many different peoples in the Andean region long before the Incas began to consolidate their empire in the 13th century AD. The Inca empire reached the height of its development in the 15th century, just 70 years before the arrival of the Spaniards in 1532. The Incas adopted Quechua as their official language in order to facilitate communication with their multilingual subjects.

Today, there are approximately 24 different dialects of Quechua, divided into regional branches known as Northern, Central and Southern Quechua. All these varieties combined are spoken by approximately eight to 10 million people, making Quechua the most widely spoken indigenous language in the Americas.

IN CASE I DON'T SEE YOU ...

The expressions *Wuynus diyas*, *Wuynas tardis* and *Wuynas nuchis*, for 'Good morning', 'Good afternoon' and 'Good evening/night', were borrowed long ago from Spanish and have become much more common than the original Quechua words.

INTRODUCTION

In this phrasebook, we use the Cuzco variety of Quechua, a southern Peruvian dialect (in the Southern Quechua linguistic branch), which is the most widely spoken in the Quechua family. It's well understood in the Peruvian departments of Apurímac, Ayacucho, Cuzco, Huancavelica and Puno, in all of Bolivia, and in the province of Santiago del Estero in Argentina, despite small differences. It can be partially understood in all other Quechua-speaking areas of the Andes, although there are some minor regional variations in pronunciation, word endings and vocabulary. You should be able to get your basic message across with Cuzco Quechua wherever you travel in the Andes.

By speaking some Quechua, you'll break down invisible barriers and show people that you have a genuine interest in their culture and language. Hearing it spoken by foreigners, however haltingly, will be appreciated by native speakers. They'll gain through seeing their language valued by visitors, and your experience will be enhanced through the goodwill shared with them.

ABBREVIATIONS USED IN THIS BOOK

adj	adjective	pl	plural
adv	adverb	prep	preposition
f	feminine	pron	pronoun
inf	infinitive	sg	singular
m	masculine	v	verb
n	noun		

PRONUNCIATION

Quechua is fairly straightforward to pronounce. Beside each word and phrase in this book, you'll find a simple pronunciation guide. It appears in colour and words are divided into syllables with a dot. The Quechua writing system is represented by italic letters.

VOWEL SOUNDS

In spoken Quechua, there are five vowel sounds that correspond to the three basic written vowels *(a, i* and *u)* of the official Quechua writing system, as approved by the Peruvian government in 1985.

Sound	Description	Quechua	
ah	as the 'a' in 'father'	*a*	
ee	as the 'ee' in 'see'	*i, iy*	
e	as the 'e' in 'bet'	*i*	(when found before or after consonants *q, q'* or *qh)*
oo	as the 'oo' in 'hoot'	*u, uw*	
o	as the 'o' in 'got'	*u*	(when found before or after consonants *q, q'* or *qh)*

Diphthongs

The Quechua writing system combines the letters *w* and *y* with *a*, *i* or *u* to form the following diphthongs (vowel sounds).

PRONUNCIATION

Sound	Description	Quechua
ow	as the 'ow' in 'vow'	*aw*
ai	as the 'ai' in 'aisle'	*ay*
yoo	as the 'u' in 'union'	*iw*
ay	as the 'ay' in 'day'	*ay* (when before or after the consonants *q, q'* or *qh*)
ui	as the 'ouie' in 'Louie'	*uy*
oy	as the 'oy' in 'toy'	*uy* (when before or after the consonants *q, q'* or *qh*)

CONSONANT SOUNDS

Most consonants are pronounced basically as they are in English. A few of the sounds are not common in English, but they shouldn't prove too difficult – the most challenging might be the 'ejective' consonants, explained on page 14.

SAY IT WITH PRIDE

According to some researchers, the term *runasimi*, roo·nah·*see*·mee, which means 'human speech', was used pejoratively by Spaniards in colonial times to distinguish 'Indian speech' from *kastillasimi*, kah·stee·lyah·*see*·mee, 'Castilian speech'. Nowadays, this term has lost these connotations and is used with pride by Quechua speakers as a name for their language.

Sound	Description	Quechua
ch	as the 'ch' in 'chew'	ch
f	as the 'f' in 'fun'	ph
g	as the 'g' in 'gun'	g
h	as the 'h' in 'hope'	h
k	as the 'k' in 'skill'	k, q
kh	as the 'ch' in the Scottish loch	k, q, p (at the end of a word)
l	as the 'l' in 'land'	l
ly	as the 'lli' in 'billion' with the middle of the tongue against the roof of the mouth	ll
m	as the 'm' in 'much'	m
n	as the 'n' in 'note'	n
ny	as the 'ny' in 'canyon'	ñ
p	as the 'p' in 'spot'	p
r	like a very short 'd' sound, not like an English 'r'	r
rr	a trilled 'r'	rr
s	as the 's' in 'saw'	s
sh	as the 'sh' in 'short'	sh
t	as the 't' in 'stop'	t
w	as the 'w' in 'wig'	w
y	as the 'y' in 'yes'	y

PRONUNCIATION

PRONUNCIATION

Aspiration & Ejectives

Aspiration refers to consonants which are pronounced with a small puff of air, as the initial 'p' in the English 'pot' (as opposed to the 'p' in 'spot' – hold your hand in front of your mouth when you say the two words and feel the difference). The meaning of a word can change depending on whether or not a consonant is aspirated. See the box on page 16 for examples of this. In our pronunciation guide, aspiration is indicated with the addition of -h. In written Quechua, aspirated consonants are indicated by the letter *h* after the initial consonant.

Symbol	Sound	Letter
ch-h	as the 'ch-h' in 'Dutch hope'	*chh*
k-h	as the 'k-h' in 'duck house'	*kh, qh*
p-h	in the Cuzco area, this sound is similar to an English 'f'; in other areas, the sound is closer to a very soft, breathy 'p'	*ph*
t-h	as the 't-h' in 'hot house'	*th*

Ejectives are consonants which are pronounced by stopping the airflow momentarily at the back of the throat and then releasing it. This is similar to the 'tt' in the cockney 'bottle', although other parts of the mouth (the lips, for example) can be used in conjunction with this throat movement to create the ejective sounds which occur in Quechua. Like aspiration, the use of ejective consonants can change the meaning of a word (see the box on page 16). In our pronunciation guide, an ejective is indicated with an apostrophe (') following the initial consonant sound.

Symbol	Sound	Letter
ch'	sharper and more abrupt than the 'ch' in 'chew'	ch'
k'	made with a click at the back of the throat	k'
p'	made by briefly closing the lips, and then 'popping' or unsticking the lips	p'
q'	made with a click in the throat like the ejective k', but strongly, at the very back of the throat	q'
t'	made with a sharp clicking of the tip of the tongue, a bit like the 'tt' in American English 'button', but more exaggerated	t'

STRESS

Words are generally stressed on the second last syllable. A stressed syllable in this book is indicated by the use of italics:

paqarichiy	pah·kah·*ree*·chee	to give life/ to establish

If the word only has two syllables, then it will be the first syllable that's stressed:

pallay	*pah*·lyai	to gather

An exception to this pattern occurs when an accent is marked over a vowel, indicating that the stress falls on that syllable:

¡achakáw!	ah·chah·*kow*!	Ouch! That's hot!
arí	ah·*ree*	yes

PRONUNCIATION

The pronunciation of aspirated and ejective consonants is one of the defining characteristics of the Cuzco, Puno and Bolivian varieties of Quechua. Be aware that these sounds alter the meaning of words, as these examples show:

chaki	chah·kee	foot/leg
ch'aki	ch'ah·kee	dry
tanta	tahn·tah	gathered together
t'anta	t'ahn·tah	bread
thanta	t-hahn·tah	old/used/worn out

If you find it difficult to make these distinctions at first, keep trying and it will come. Don't worry too much if you do make a mistake though – your meaning will often be clear from the context.

INTONATION

Intonation patterns in Quechua vary from those of English in one very important way – questions have the same intonation as statements (in Quechua, essentially a falling one). Instead of a rising intonation, specific question words or prefixes indicate that a question is being asked. Quechua also uses a different way of expressing exclamation – the intonation doesn't actually change, instead there is an increased stress on the syllable that emphasises the statement.

GRAMMAR

This chapter is one of the few overviews of Quechua grammar you'll see. It's not exhaustive, but it will give you enough of a foundation to understand the basic structure of the language so you can construct simple sentences of your own.

In Quechua, sentences are built around basic root words, and the rest of the meaning is added to the sentence by attaching suffixes. In this chapter, to make it easier to distinguish root words from their suffixes, we have used a hyphen between the root and each suffix. The root word always comes first.

There are no irregular verbs in Quechua – all Quechua verbs follow the rules according to each tense. The tenses presented in this phrasebook are the most essential ones.

The following abbreviations are used in this chapter:

adj	adjective	n	noun
assert	assertive	neg	negative
emph	emphatic	obj	object
excl	exclusive 'we'	obl	obligation
fut	future tense	past	past tense
imp	imperative	poss	possessive
incl	inclusive 'we'	pres	present tense
int	interrogative	top	topic
interj	interjection/	uncert	uncertainty
	exclamation	v	verb
lit	literal translation		

WORD ORDER

In general, the basic sentence word order in Quechua is subject-object-verb:

> Satuku is eating bread.   *Satuku t'anta-ta-n mikhu-sha-n.*
>   (lit: Satuku bread-obj-assert eating-is)

Note that the assertive suffix indicates that the speaker is stating something from personal experience. See the full explanation on page 22.

Because of the nature of a suffix-based system, word order is quite flexible. You can put any word first to emphasise it:

> Satuku is eating *bread*.   *T'anta-ta-n Satuku mikhu-sha-n.*
>   (lit: bread-obj-assert Satuku eating-is)

Here it's 'bread' that's emphasised.

ARTICLES

There's no word for 'the', but 'a/an' is *huq* (literally 'one'). It can also mean 'some' when used with a plural noun:

> a restaurant   *huq mikhuna wasi*   (lit: one food house)
>
> some people   *huq runa-kuna*   (lit: one person-pl)

ROOT WORDS

Root words are the building blocks of a sentence, onto which suffixes are attached to create the full meaning.

SUFFIXES

Suffixes do the functional work in a sentence, showing how the various root words work together to give meaning. For instance, *wasi*, 'house', is a noun, but by adding the suffixes *-cha* (which changes certain nouns to verbs) and *-y* (which marks the infinitive), it becomes the verb *wasi-cha-y*, 'to build (a house)'.

Dependent Suffixes

Dependent suffixes can only be used with certain parts of speech or parts of a sentence: they add meaning to a word. An example in English would be the prefix 'un-', as in 'unusual': it cannot be used on its own, but when combined with other words, it carries a distinct meaning (it creates the oposite of the word).

There are three major groups of dependent suffixes:

1. The **nominals** are used only with nouns and pronouns and include the subject marker, object marker, number markers, possessives and several prepositions.

2. The **verbals** are used only with verbs. These include tense, mood and command markers. See Verb page 32.

3. The **derivational suffixes** change one part of speech to another. They have a parallel in English: eg, by adding '-ness', the adjective 'sad' can be turned into the noun 'sadness'. Each specific derivational suffix can only be attached to a specific part of speech, eg, the suffix *-sqa* can only be added to a verb to form an adjective, never to form a noun (see the table below).

to get tired (v)	*sayk'u-y*	tired (adj)		*sayk'u-sqa*
to sit down (v)	*tiya-y*	seat; place to sit (n)		*tiya-na*
head (n)	*uma*	big-headed (adj)		*uma-sapa*
stone (n)	*rumi*	to change to stone (v)		*rumi-ya-y*
little (adj)	*pisi*	scarcity (n)		*pisi-y*
hot (adj)	*rupha*	to burn (v)		*rupha-chi-y*

GRAMMAR

Here are some examples of nominal dependent suffixes, and their uses:

because of/due to/ on behalf of	*-rayku*
I came to Cuzco because of the Inti Raymi Festival.	*Inti Raymi-rayku-n Qusqu-man hamurqa-ni.* (lit: Inti Raymi-because_ of-assert Cuzco-to came-I)

for (the purpose of)	*-paq*
I work for my family.	*Ayllu-y-paq llank'a-ni.* (lit: family-my-for work-I)

from *-manta*	
She/He is returning from Potosí.	*Putusi llaqta-manta kutimu-sha-n.* (lit: Potosí city-from return-ing-she/he)

in (location)	*-pi*
I work in Chinchero.	*Chinchiru-pi llank'a-ni.* (lit: Chinchero-in work-I)

possessive ('s)	*-q/-pa* (after vowel/consonant)
man's	*qhari-q* (lit: man-of)

until *-kama*	
The road goes to Machu Picchu.	*Machu Pikchu-kama ñan ri-sha-n.* (lit: Machu Picchu-until road go-ing-it)

with *-wan*	
They're talking with the police.	*Wardiya-wan rima-sha-nku.* (lit: police-with talk-ing-they)

GRAMMAR

MULTI-FUNCTION SUFFIXES: -TA & -MAN

The suffix *-ta* is can serve numerous functions within a sentence, including:

- object marker, direct and indirect

  I see him.   *Pay-**ta** qhawa-ni.*
                                (lit: he-obj see-I)

  Can you help me   *¿Yanapa-wanki-man-chu qipiy-**ta***
     find my backpack?   *maskhay-**ta**?*
                                (lit: help-me-could-int
                                    backpack-obj look_for-obj)

Note that as an indirect object *-ta* can only be used with verbs that don't involve movement of the direct object (see second example). The two verbs – help and find – don't involve movement of the direct object 'backpack'.

- destination, meaning 'to(wards)'

  I'm going to Apurimac.   *Apurimaq-**ta** ri-sha-ni.*
                                (lit: Apurimac-to go-ing-I)

- derivational suffix, changing adjectives to adverbs

  good   *allin*

  He does well.   *Allin-**ta** ruwa-n.*
                                (lit: good-adv do-he)

  Here, the two functions of object marker and destination come together in one sentence:

  I want to go   *Apurimaq-**ta** riy-**ta** muna-ni.*
     to Apurimac.   (lit: Apurimac-to go-obj want-I)

continues on next page

MULTI-FUNCTION SUFFIXES: -TA & -MAN

continues from previous page

The suffix *-man* is similar to *-ta* in that it serves as both an object and destination marker (also meaning 'to(wards)'). Its function as object marker, however, is limited to indirect objects only. It's applied in cases where verbs involving movement are used, and in connection with a concrete noun or the pronoun *pay*.

I give him money.	*Qulqi-ta pay-man qu-ni.* (lit: money-obj he-obj give-I)
to/towards	*-man*

This bus is going
   to Ecuador.
	Ikwadur suyu-man
	kay uniwus ri-sha-n.
	(lit: Ecuador region-to this bus
	   go-ing-it)

GRAMMAR

Independent Suffixes

The use of independent suffixes is not limited to a particular part of speech. These are attached to the key word in the sentence (which can be any part of speech) but express the speaker's attitude to the whole sentence.

Assertion

The suffix *-n/-mi* (after vowel/consonant respectively) indicates that the speaker is stating something from personal experience.

I speak English.	*Nuqa inlis-ta-n rima-ni.* (lit: I English-obj-assert speak-I)
My stomach hurts.	*Wiksa-y-mi nana-wa-sha-n.* (lit: stomach-my-assert hurt- to_me-ing-it)

Hearsay

The suffix *-s/-si* (after vowel/consonant respectively) indicates that the speaker knows the information second-hand.

People say that village is far away.	*Chay llaqta sinchi karu-s.* (lit: that village very far-hearsay)
People say that she/he speaks Quechua.	*Pay-si runasimi-ta rima-n.* (lit: she/he-hearsay Quechua-obj speak-she/he)

Uncertainty

The suffix *-ch/-cha* (after vowel/consonant) indicates uncertainty over the veracity or validity of words.

He probably speaks Quechua.	*Pay-cha runasimi-ta rima-n.* (lit: he-uncert Quechua-obj speak-he)
There are probably sandals in that store.	*Chay tinda-pi-ch usut'a-kuna ka-n.* (lit: that store-in-uncert sandal-pl there_is-it)

Topic Marker

The suffix *-qa* is an important independent suffix because it marks the repetition of the topic – or main idea or subject – in the conversation. It's therefore referred to as a topic marker.

You don't need to use this suffix the first time you mention a specific subject in a conversation, but after that you must add it to the end of that subject (after all other suffixes, if any exist):

Your brother is sick.	*Turay-ki unqu-shan-mi.*
He can't go to Quito.	*Manan pay-qa Kitu-ta riy-ta ati-n-chu.* (lit: brother-your sick-is-assert. no he-top Quito-obj go-to can-he-neg)

Emphasis

The emphatic suffix *-má* is used to express surprise, to correct someone else's statement, to correct oneself, or to simply emphasise a point. It's always the final suffix to be added to a word, and is stressed:

He came all the way   *¡Quchapampa-manta-má*
    from Cochabamba!   *kuti-rqa-mu-n!*
                           (lit: Cochabamba-from-emph
                               come_back-past-to-here-he!)

Others

Other important independent suffixes are *-chu*, used to mark questions or negatives (see Questions on page 39), *-pis/-pas*, meaning 'and/also/too' (see Conjunctions on page 42) and *-ña*, meaning 'already'.

I already did it.   *Tuku-rqu-ni-ña-n.*
                        (lit: finish-just-I-already-assert)

NOUNS

Nouns are root words (see Root Words, page 18). In general, a noun is expressed as a simple singular entity. If you want to make it plural or modify it in any other way, you do so through the use of specific suffixes.

WE X TWO

It's important to note that, unlike English, Quechua has two categories of the first person plural (we/us). The inclusive category includes the speaker, the listener and anyone else to whom the speaker is referring ('you, me and everyone'). The exclusive category includes the speaker and anyone else to whom she or he is referring, but not the listener ('me and the others, but not you').

Plurals

To make plural nouns, simply add the suffix *-kuna*. Note, however, that if a specific number or quantity of something is mentioned, the plural suffix does not need to be added. (See Numbers, page 167, for more on this.)

store	*tinda*
stores	*tinda-kuna* (lit: store-pl)
one boat	*huq wampu* (lit: one boat)
ten boats	*chunka wampu* (lit: ten boat)

Gender

Quechua does not express gender for inanimate objects, only for animals and people. To indicate gender for people, use *warmi*, 'woman', or *qhari*, 'man'. If the gender of an animal is relevant, you have to specifically identify it as *china*, 'female', or *urqu*, 'male'. So a 'female dog' would be *china alqu* and a 'male dog' *urqu alqu*.

Some words borrowed from Spanish explicitly indicate gender, such as *awilu*, 'grandfather', and *awila*, 'grandmother'.

PRONOUNS
Subject Pronouns

Subject pronouns can be expressed with individual words as well as with suffixes. If the context of a sentence makes clear who or what the subject is, the pronoun is not required. The suffixes often provide all the information necessary. These are the individual subject pronouns:

SINGULAR		PLURAL	
I	*nuqa*	we (incl)	*nuqanchis*
		we (excl)	*nuqayku*
you (sg)	*qan*	you (pl)	*qankuna*
she/he	*pay*	they	*paykuna*

GRAMMAR

Subject/Object Pronoun Suffixes

As with just about everything else in Quechua, personal pronouns are expressed through the use of suffixes which identify both the subject and object in a sentence. These suffixes, however, are attached to the verb and are compulsory in the sentence. The pronoun suffixes change depending on verb tense.

> I give you money.   *Nuqa qulqi-ta qu-yki.*
> (lit: I money-obj give-I_
> to_ you_sg_obj_pres)

Suffixes for Present Tense

Singular

Subject \ Object	me	you	her/him
I	-	-yki	-
you	-wanki	-	-
she/he	-wan	-sunki	-
we (incl)	-	-	-
we (excl)	-	-ykiku	-
you	-wankichis	-	-
they	-wanku	-sunkiku	-

Plural

Subject \ Object	us (incl)	us (excl)	you	them
I	-	-	-ykichis	-
you	-	-wankiku	-	-
she/he	-wanchis	-wanku	-sunkichis	-
we (incl)	-	-	-	-
we (excl)	-	-	-ykiku	-
you	-	-wankiku	-	-
they	-wanchis	-wanku	-sunkichis	-

There's a different suffix for each subject/object combination and for each tense of the verb. Here, the suffix *-yki* indicates the subject, object and tense of the verb at the one time.

I give you (sg) beer.   *Aha-ta qu-yki.*
                             (lit: beer-obj give-I_to_
                             you_sg_obj_pres)

The following tables show possible subject/object combinations. Some subject/object pronoun combinations are not logically possible in Quechua, so are indicated by empty cells.

Suffixes for Past Tense

Singular

Subject \ Object	me	you	her/him
I	-	-rqayki	-
you	-warqanki	-	-
she/he	-warqan	-rqasunki	-
we (incl)	-	-	-
we (excl)	-	-rqaykiku	-
you	-warqankichis	-	-
they	-warqanku	-rqasunkiku	-

Plural

Subject \ Object	us (incl)	us (excl)	you	them
I	-	-	-rqaykichis	-
you	-	-warqankiku	-	-
she/he	-warqanchis	-warqanku	-rqasunkichis	-
we (incl)	-	-	-	-
we (excl)	-	-	-rqaykiku	-
you	-	-warqankiku	-	-
they	-warqanchis	-warqanku	-rqasunkichis	-

GRAMMAR

Note that for the third person (sg/pl) there are no specific object pronoun suffixes. Instead, you'd use the subject pronoun *pay(kuna)* (see page 25) plus the indirect object marker *-man* to express the object 'to him/her/them'. You then add the appropriate subject pronoun suffix to the verb (*-ni* in the example):

Suffixes for Future Tense

Singular

Object Subject	me	you	her/him
I	-	-sayki	-
you	-wanki	-	-
she/he	-wanqa	-sunki	-
we (incl)	-	-	-
we (excl)	-	-saykiku	-
you	-wankichis	-	-
they	-wanqaku	-sunkiku	-

Plural

Object Subject	us (incl)	us (excl)	you	them
I	-	-	-saykichis	-
you	-	-wankiku	-	-
she/he	-wasunchis	-wanqaku	-sunkichis	-
we (incl)	-	-	-	-
we (excl)	-	-	-saykiku	-
you	-	-wankiku	-	-
they	-wasunchis	-wanqaku	-sunkichis	-

I give them sweets.	*Nuqa miski'i-ta paykuna-man qu-ni.* (lit: I sweet-obj them-obj give-I)

ADJECTIVES

Adjectives come before nouns. Only the nouns are pluralised, not the adjectives.

beautiful day	*sumaq p'unchay*	(lit: pretty day)
black donkeys	*yana asnu-kuna*	(lit: black donkey-pl)

Kusi is buying some beautiful clothes.	*Kusi sumaq p'achakuna-ta ranti-sha-n.*
	(lit: Kusi beautiful clothes-obj buy-ing-he)

The concept of 'very' can be indicated by repeating the adjective, as in:

very far away	*karu karu*	(lit: far far)
very big	*hatun hatun*	(lit: big big)

Comparatives

In Quechua, *aswan*, 'more', and *pisi*, 'less', are placed in front of the adjective to make a comparison:

big	*hatun*	
bigger	*aswan hatun*	(lit: more big)
smaller	*pisi hatun*	(lit: less big)

It's also very common for either the emphatic suffix *-má* (see page 24) or the assertive suffix *-n/-mi* to be added to the end of the adjective as well:

I'm younger than him.	*Pay-manta aswan wayna-má ka-ni.*
	(lit: she/he-from more young-emph am-I)

Superlatives

The superlative is expressed using 'the most', *lliw-manta aswan ...-n/-mi*, or 'the least', *lliw-manta aswan pisi ...-n/-mi*. The blank is filled in by an adjective:

This town is the
    biggest.

Kay llaqta-qa lliw-manta aswan hatun-mi.
(lit: this town-top all-from more big-assert)

That town is the
    smallest.

Chay llaqta-qa lliw-manta aswan pisi hatun-mi.
(lit: that town-top all-from more less big-assert)

ADVERBS

Adverbs can be either words derived from adjectives through the use of the adverb marker *-ta* (like adding '-ly' in English), or independent root words. Here are some common adverbs:

easily	*chhalla-lla/phasil-cha-lla*
in this way/manner	*hina*
quickly/rapidly	*usqhay(-lla)*
slowly/carefully	*alli-lla-manta*
very	*ancha/sinchi/nishu*
well	*allin-ta/kusa*

All of the above are 'stand-alone' root words, although some of them carry suffixes to make them adverbs.

DEMONSTRATIVES

In Quechua, words like 'this', 'that', 'these' and 'those' can be adjectives when describing a noun, as in *kay qhatu*, 'this market', or pronouns when replacing a noun if it has already been mentioned:

This town is lovely,   ***Kay** llaqta sumaq-mi,*
   that one is not.   *chay-qa manan sumaq-chu.*
                              (lit: this town beautiful-assert,
                                 that-top not beautiful-neg)

There's no difference between singular and plural demonstrative adjectives in Quechua, since it's the noun and not the adjective that is pluralised. Demonstrative pronouns add the suffix *-kuna* to pluralise: eg, *kay-kuna*, literally 'this-plural', thus 'these'.

However, a distinction is made between three – rather than only two – degrees of distance:

this/these   *kay/ankay*
that/those (closer to listener) *chay/anchay*
that/those (further away   *chaqay/chhaqay/haqay*
   from listener and speaker)

The second form of 'that/those' does not really have an equivalent in English.

This boat is going   ***Kay** wampu-qa*
   to Puno.   *Punu-man-mi ri-sha-n.*
                              (lit: this boat-top
                                 Puno-to-assert go-ing-it)

Those boats over there   ***Chaqay** wampu-kuna*
   are small.   *huch'uy-mi.*
                              (lit: that boat-pl small-assert)

A BEAUTIFUL DESIRE TO LOVE

Muna-y is a very versatile word, meaning 'to like,' as well as 'to love', 'to desire'; 'to want' and 'to need'. As an adjective, it can mean 'good', 'beautiful' or 'lovely', and as a noun, 'desire' 'love' or 'goodwill'.

GRAMMAR

POSSESSIVES

Possession in Quechua is shown by adding a possessive suffix to the noun being possessed. You can also add a possessive pronoun when you want to clarify the possession. The possessive pronouns consist of subject pronouns with the suffixes *-q* and *-pa* added (after vowel/consonant). The suffixes are the essential elements for showing possession and are added to the nouns right after the root word, whereas possessive pronouns are mostly used for emphasis.

I just found my backpack.	*Qipi-y-ta tari-rqu-ni-n.* (lit: backpack-my-obj find-just-I-assert)
These skirts are ours.	*Nuqanchis-pa-n kay pullira-kuna-qa.* (lit: ours-assert this skirt-pl-top)

VERBS

Verbs will always have at least one suffix. This obligatory suffix will show what tense (past, present or future) the verb is in, and who or what the subject of the verb is, ie first, second or third person, singular or plural. The suffix *-y* indicates the infinitive of the verb, eg, *ka-y*, 'to be', and this form is used in the dictionaries.

Possessive Pronoun		Possessive Suffix	
nuqa-q	mine	*-y*	my
qan-pa	yours (sg)	*-yki*	your (sg)
pay-pa	hers/his	*-n*	her/his
nuqanchis-pa	ours (incl)	*-nchis*	our (incl)
nuqayku-q	ours (excl)	*-yku*	our (excl)
qankuna-q	yours (pl)	*-ykichis*	your (pl)
paykuna-q	theirs	*-nku*	their

GRAMMAR

Present Tense

The present tense is used either to indicate an action that occurs once in the present, or to indicate habitual actions. To form it, simply add the appropriate subject pronoun suffix (see Pronoun Suffixes page 26) to the verb root.

Remember that the subject pronoun suffix is essential, but the subject pronoun in parentheses is optional.

I speak Quechua. *Nuqa runasimi-ta rima-**ni**.*
(lit: I Quechua-obj speak-I)

Person	Subject Pronoun	Object ('Quechua')	Obj Suffix	Verb Root ('to speak')	Subject Pron Suffix
	(Nuqa)	*runasimi*	*-ta*	*rima*	*-ni*
ou (sg)	*(Qan)*				*-nki*
he/he	*(Pay)*				*-n*
ve (incl)	*(Nuqanchis)*				*-nchis*
ve (excl)	*(Nuqayku)*				*-yku*
ou (pl)	*(Qankuna)*				*-nkichis*
ney	*(Paykuna)*				*-nku*

To express an action that's in the process of happening (like the '-ing' form in English), insert the suffix *-sha* between the verb root and the subject pronoun suffix:

She's/He's speaking *Pay runasimi-ta rima-**sha**-n.*
Quechua. (lit: she/he Quechua-obj
speak-ing-she/he_pres)

Past Tense

To form the past tense, add the suffix *-rqa* in front of the subject pronoun suffix. Note that in the past tense, the suffix *-n* for the third person singular is optional.

Person	Subject Pronoun	Object ('Quechua')	Obj Suffix	Verb Root ('to speak')	Past Suffix	Subject Pron Suf
I	*(Nuqa)*	*inlis*	*-ta*	*rima*	*-rqa*	*-ni*
you (sg)	*(Qan)*					*-nki*
she/he	*(Pay)*					*(-n)*
we (incl)	*(Nuqanchis)*					*-nchis*
we (excl)	*(Nuqayku)*					*-yku*
you (pl)	*(Qankuna)*					*-nkichi*
they (pl)	*(Paykuna)*					*-nku*

She/He spoke English.   *Pay inlis-ta rima-rqa-(n).*
(lit: she/he English-obj speak-past-(she/he_pres))

Future Tense

The future tense is used primarily to express simple future actions ('I'll come tomorrow.'/'Will you come tomorrow?') and probability when used with the 'uncertainty' validator *-ch/-cha* (after vowel/consonant).

In the future tense, most subject pronoun suffixes change form rather than adding yet another suffix to show the tense. Two subject pronoun suffixes, however, remain the same as in the present tense: the singular and plural forms of 'you', *-nki* (sg) and *-nkichis* (pl). When these appear, you'll need to judge by the context whether the speaker refers to the present or the future.

I'll speak Spanish.   *Nuqa kastillanu-ta rima-saq.*
(lit: I Spanish-obj speak-I_fut)

Person	Subject Pronoun	Object ('Spanish')	Obj Suffix	Verb Root ('to speak')	Subject Pron Suffix & Future Tense
I	(Nuqa)				-saq
you (sg)	(Qan)				-nki
she/he	(Pay)	kastillanu	-ta	rima	-nqa
we (incl)	(Nuqanchis)				-sunchis
we (excl)	(Nuqayku)				-saqku
you (pl)	(Qankuna)				-nkichis
they	(Paykuna)				-nqaku

They will speak Spanish.   *Paykuna kastillanu-ta rima-nqaku.*
(lit: they Spanish-obj speak-they_fut)

Imperative

The imperative is a direct command which tells your listener to do something. This is indicated by the suffix *-y:*

Come here!   *¡Hamu-y!*
(lit: come-imp)

In the case of a negative command, the sentence begins with *ama* and the suffix *-chu* is added to the verb as the last suffix:

Don't do that!   *¡Ama chay-ta ruwa-y-chu!*
(lit: don't that-obj do-imp-neg)

(See also Modals, page 37.)

GRAMMAR

To Be

The verb **ka-y** means 'to be', in the sense of 'to exist', and is also used to describe something or someone, as in *Nuqa turista-n ka-ni,* 'I'm a tourist' (lit: I tourist-assert am-I). **Ka-y** can also mean 'there is/are' when stating something.

Don't confuse the verb **ka-y**, with the demonstrative adjective *kay*, 'this', which has the same spelling (see Demonstratives page 31).

You (sg) are a pretty girl.	*Qan sumaq warma-cha-n ka-nki.* (lit: you-sg beautiful girl-little-assert are-you)
She's/He's on the train.	*Pay trin-pi-n ka-sha-n.* (lit: she/he train-in-assert be-ing-she/he)
We (incl) are tired.	*Nuqanchis sayk'usqa-n ka-nchis.* (lit: we incl tired-assert are-we_incl)
They're in Coricancha.	*Paykuna Qurikancha-pi-n ka-sha-nku.* (lit: they Coricancha-in-assert be-ing-they)
There are a lot of mountains around this town.	*Kay llaqta-pi askha urqu-kuna-n ka-nku.* (lit: this town-in many mountain-pl-assert are-they)

Note that when defining someone or something in the third person, you don't use the verb *ka-y* (or any other verb):

She's/He's a foreigner.	*Pay hawa runa-n.* (lit: she/he outside_person-assert)
They're healers.	*Paykuna hampiq-mi.* (lit: they healer-assert)

To Have

The verb *ka-y*, 'to be', also serves the function of the English 'to have' in the sense of possession. Literally, it points out something that is or isn't in someone's possession:

Do you have children?	*¿Ka-n-chu wawa-yki?* (lit: there_is-she/he-int child-your)
Yes, I do.	*Arí, ka-n-mi.* (lit: yes there_is-she/he-assert)
No, I don't.	*Mana-n ka-n-chu.* (lit: no-assert there_is-she/ he-neg)
I have a house.	*Wasi-yuq-mi ka-ni.* (lit: house-with-assert am-I)

MODALS

Modals modify the meaning of other verbs in a sentence. They express ability, necessity, desire or need, as in 'can read', 'need to go' and 'want to drink'. As you'd expect, modals also take the form of suffixes.

Must; Should

The simple suffix *-na* plus the appropriate possessive suffix (see Possessives page 32) added to the verb, in that order, indicates the notion of 'must' in Quechua. You can also use the verb *ka-y*, 'to have', which is used only when the obligation implied is unavoidable ('have to') – in which case the progressive form of the present tense *ka-sha-n* (see page 33) is recommended. When the obligation implied is avoidable (eg, 'should' or 'ought to'), the verb *ka-y* is not used.

Must; Have To; Need To

I have to work.	*Llank'a-na-y ka-sha-n.* (lit: work-obl-my be-ing-it)
We (excl) have to leave.	*Lluqsi-na-yku ka-sha-n.* (lit: leave-obl-our be-ing-it)

GRAMMAR

Ought To; Should

I should eat.

Mikhu-na-y.
(lit: eat-obl-my)

We (incl) ought to rest.

Sama-na-nchis.
(lit: rest-obl-our_incl)

Can; To be Able

The verb *ati-y* meaning 'to be able/to have the ability' is used in a similar way as its English counterpart:

They can dance.

Paykuna tusu-y-ta ati-nku.
(lit: they dance-inf-obj can-
they_pres)

Must Not; Cannot

Use the negative command form (see Imperatives, page 35). Quechua speakers would typically just say *Ama chay unu-ta ukyay-chu,* 'Don't drink that water' (lit: don't that water-obj drink-neg).

Like

Muna-y is the verb for 'to like' in Quechua. It can be used by itself or with another verb:

I like Cuzco.

Nuqa Qusqu-ta muna-ni.
(lit: I Cuzco-obj like-I)

We (excl) like to
buy clothes.

*Nuqayku p'acha-ta
ranti-y-ta muna-yku.*
(lit: we clothes-obj
buy-inf-obj like-we_excl)

QUESTIONS
'Yes/No' Questions

To ask a 'yes/no' question, add the independent suffix *-chu* to the most relevant word in the question. Note that the question marker is on the verb:

Are you (sg) married? *¿Kasaru-chu ka-nki?*
(lit: married-int are-you_sg)

The suffix can also be attached to the noun (or to adjectives or adverbs if those are the elements being questioned):

Are you going to *¿Quchapampa-ta-chu*
Cochabamba? *ri-sha-nki?*
(lit: Cochabamba-obj-int
go-ing-you)

You can answer 'yes/no' questions either with *arí,* 'yes', or *mana,* 'no'. If, in an affirmative answer, you repeat the entire question, the assertive suffix *-n/-mi* (after vowel/consonant) needs to be attached to the most relevant word. When repeating the question in a negative answer, the suffix *-chu* is attached to the most relevant word, while the assertive suffix is attached to the word *mana,* 'no', becoming *mana-n*.

Are you (sg) married? *¿Kasaru-chu ka-nki?*
(lit: married-int are-you_sg)

Yes, I'm married. *Arí, kasaru-n ka-ni.*
(lit: yes married-assert be-I)

No, I'm not married. *Mana-n kasaru-chu ka-ni.*
(lit: no-assert married-neg be-I)

Question Words

What?	¿Ima?
What's that?	¿Ima-taq chay? ¿Ima-n chay?
Who?	¿Pi?
Who's that woman?	¿Pi-taq chay warmi?
Whose?	¿Pi-q?
Whose car is that?	¿Pi-q-taq chay awtu?
Where?	¿May?
Where are you going?	¿May-ta-n ri-sha-nki?
Where are you from?	¿May-manta-n ka-nki?
Which?	¿Mayqin?
Which market do you like?	¿Mayqin qhatu-ta-taq muna-nki?
How?	¿Imayna?
How are you?	¿Imayna-taq ka-sha-nki?
How much?/How many?	¿Hayk'a?
How much is that bag, Madam?	¿Hayk'a-taq chay waya-qa, mamitáy?
When?	¿Hayk'aq?
When are we going?	¿Hayk'aq-mi ripu-ku-sun?
Why?	¿Imarayku?/¿Imanaqtin?/¿Imanasqa?
Why is there no car?	¿Imarayku-n mana karru ka-nchu?

Information Questions

With all standard question words, the final suffix *-n/-mi* or *-taq* should be added. If in doubt about endings, use *-taq*.

NEGATIVES

There are two words to express negation. The first one is *mana* (or *mana-n* when asserting something), 'no/not', in conjunction with the negative suffix *-chu*. The second one is *ama*, 'don't', used in negative commands (see Imperatives page 35). Both of them are placed at the beginning of a sentence, while the placement of the suffix *-chu* varies as it's attached to the most relevant word of the sentence.

I don't speak Quechua.	*(Nuqa) mana-n runasimi-ta rima-ni-chu.*
	(lit: I no-assert Quechua-obj speak-I-neg)
Don't travel alone.	*Ama sapalla-yki puri-y-chu.*
	(lit: don't alone-you_sg travel-imp-neg)

PREPOSITIONS

Prepositions are expressed through certain dependent suffixes as well as some individual words. For more information, see Suffixes, page 18.

after	*chaymanta/hinaspa/qhipata*
among	*-pura*
because (of)	*-rayku*
during	*-pi*
for	*-paq*
from	*-manta*
in (location)	*-pi*
to/towards	*-man*
until (time/place)	*-kama*
with	*-wan*
without ...	*mana ...-yuq*
	(used with a noun only)

GRAMMAR

CONJUNCTIONS

Conjunctions are words or phrases that join concepts or parts of sentences.

In Quechua, most conjunctions are individual words rather than suffixes, but there's one exception: *-pis* or *-pas* (used interchangeably) meaning 'also/and/too'. This suffix is added to verbs or nouns as the very last suffix.

You can go to Arequipa by car and by train.	*Karru-wan-**pis** trin-wan-**pis** runa-kuna Arikipa-ta ri-nku.* (lit: car-with-and train-with-and person-pl Arequipa-to go-they)
Me too.	*Nuqa-**pis**.* (lit: I-too)

after(wards)	*chay-qa/chay-man/chay-pa/ qhipa-n-ta*
and/too/also	*-pis/-pas*
because	*-rayku*
but	*icha-qa*
even so/then	*chay-pacha-pas*
finally	*tuku-na-paq-taq/p'uchuka-y-pi*
first (of all)	*ñawpa-q(-ta)*
however	*chay-puwan-pas*
instead	*aswan(-pas)*
nevertheless	*chay-puwan-pas*
next	*chay-qa/chay-man/chay-pa/ qhipa-n-ta*
or	*icha/utaq*
rather	*aswan(-pas)/icha-qa*
so/therefore	*chay-rayku/nis-paqa/chay-mi*

GRAMMAR

MEETING PEOPLE

When initiating conversations in Quechua, you should be aware that since the time of the Conquest, Spanish speakers have often considered themselves superior to Quechua speakers. One form of discrimination has been a refusal by Spanish speakers to use Quechua at all. If you're in a monolingual Quechua community, there'll be no problem with jumping right in, but if in doubt, try asking in Spanish first:

> Do you speak Quechua?
> ¿Habla usted Quechua?   hah·blah oo·sted ke·chwa?

YOU SHOULD KNOW

		YACHANAYKIN
Yes.	ah·*ree*	*Arí.*
No.	*mah*·nah	*Mana.*
Please.	ah·*lyee*·choo	*Allichu.*
Thank you.	sool·*pai*·kee	*Sulpayki.*

GREETINGS & GOODBYES
NAPAYKUYKUNAPAS KACHARPARIKUNAPAS

Greetings and farewells are essential elements of social interaction, and you'll be considered rude if you don't use them. Both greetings and goodbyes should be accompanied by a handshake or a hug. When saying goodbye, a simple wave of the hand is appropriate when you're already at a distance.

Good morning.	*wee·noos dee·*ahs	*Wuynus diyas.*
Good day. (noon)	*ah·*lyeen *p'oon·*chai;	*Allin p'unchay;*
	*ah·*lyeen *p'oon·*chow	*Allin p'unchaw.*
Good afternoon.	*wee·*nahs *tahr·*dis	*Wuynas tardis.*
Good evening/	*wee·*nahs *noo·*chis;	*Wuynas nuchis;*
night.	*ah·*lyeen *too·*tah	*Allin tuta.*
Hello/Hi.	ree·mai·koo·*lyai·*kee/	*Rimaykullayki/*
	nah·pai·koo·*lyai·*kee	*Napaykullayki.*
Goodbye.	hokh koo·tee·*kah·*mah;	*Huq kutikama;*
	too·pah·nahn·chees·	*Tupananchis-*
	*kah·*mah	*kama.*
Bye.	rah·too·*kah·*mah	*Ratukama.*

CIVILITIES   YUPAYCHAKUYKUNA

The Quechua people are generally friendly, helpful, respectful
people. Reciprocity is a very important feature of good manners
in the Andes. If you ask something of someone, you should be
willing to offer in return a small gift, like a souvenir from your
home country, or a tip.

Please.	ah·*lyee·*choo	*Allichu.*
Thank you	ah·nyai·*chai·*kee/	*Añaychayki/*
(very much).	sool·*pai·*kee	*Sulpayki*
	(ahn·*chah·*tah)	*(anchata)*
	ah·grah·dee·*see·*kee	*agradisiyki.*
You're welcome.	ee·mah·*mahn·*tah;	*Imamanta;*
	*mah·*nah	*Mana*
	ee·mah·mahn·*tah·*pahs	*imamantapas.*
Excuse me.	dees·peen·sah·*yoo·*wai	*Dispinsayuway.*
Sorry.	pahm·pah·chah·*yoo·*wai	*Pampachayuway.*

FORMS OF ADDRESS

IMAHINA RUNAKUNA NINAKUSQAN

In Quechua, different forms of address represent different degrees of familiarity, or the age of the person being addressed.

As a foreigner in Quechua-speaking territory, the safest form of address for you to use with a Quechua speaker is *Tayta*, tai·tah, or *taytáy*, tai·tai, 'Sir/Mister' for men, and *Mama*, mah·mah, or *mamáy*, mah·mai, 'Madam/Mrs' for women, followed by their first name if you know it: *Tayta Satuku* or *Mama Marsilina*.

Madam/Mrs	*mah*·mah/mah·*mai*/ mah·mah·*lyai*/ mah·mee·*tai*/ *doo*·nyah/see·*nyoo*·rah	*Mama/mamáy/ mamallay/ mamitáy/ Duña/Siñura*
Sir/Mr	*tai*·tah/tai·*tai*/ tai·tah·*lyai*/pah·*pai*/ wee·rah·*ko*·chah/ doon/*see*-nyoor	*Tayta/taytáy/ taytalláy/papáy/ Wiraqucha/ Dun/Siñur*

Note that if you're writing to someone, the forms *Duña, Siñura, Mama* for women and *Dun, Siñur, Tayta* and *Wiraqucha* for men, all have a capital. While *Mama* and *Tayta* must be used with a proper name, *Wiraqucha* can also be used without one. The forms *mamáy, mamalláy, mamitáy, taytáy, taytalláy* and *papáy* are not used with proper names.

FOR THE PEOPLE

Many Quechua speakers call themselves *runa*, roo·nah, which means 'the people'. The Spanish terms *indio/ india* (m/f) or *cholo/chola* (m/f) are used by some Latin Americans to refer to the indigenous people. These names are derogatory, so don't use them. Instead, use the Spanish *indígena*, 'indigenous person' or *campesino/campesina* (m/f), meaning 'a farmer/farm labourer; a person living in a rural area'.

MEETING PEOPLE

Miss

to a young woman	*see*·pahs/*p'ahs*·nyah	*sipas/p'asña*
to a girl	*see·pahs*·chah/	*sipascha/*
	p'ahs·*nyah*·chah	*p'asñacha*

young man

to an adolescent	*mahkh*·t'ah	*maqt'a*
to a young boy	mahkh·*t'ah*·chah	*maqt'acha*
little girl/boy	wahr·*mah*·chah	*warmacha*

APOLOGIES

PAMPACHAYKUNA

Excuse me. (apology)
  pahm·pah·chah·*yoo*·wai/
  dees·peen·sah·*yoo*·wai

Pampachayuway/
Dispinsayuway.

Excuse me. (to get past)
  pah·sai·*koo*·sahkh

Pasaykusaq.

It's OK. Never mind.
  ah·*lyeen*·mee.
  ah·mah lyah·kee·*kui*·choo

Allinmi.
Ama llakikuychu.

HEY YOU!

¡Yaw!, yow! , is an informal way to attract someone's attention, similar to 'Hey!' in English. It's usually combined with someone's name or one of the forms of address we've mentioned. It would be considered rude to use it with an adult, or someone you don't know.

People may call you *ringu/gringu* (m), *reen*·goo/ green·goo , 'gringo', or *ringa/gringa* (f), *reen*·gah/ green·gah , 'gringa', if they don't know your name. In recent decades in Latin America, these terms have lost their derogatory connotations, and are now terms of respect. If someone knows your name, they might preface it with *Dun/Siñur/Tayta/Wiraqucha* (m) or *Duña/Siñura* (f) – all terms that refer to pale-skinned foreigners.

BODY LANGUAGE

ÑAWIWAN, MAKIWAN, UMAWAN RIMAY

Quechua speakers are generally humble and may not look you in the eye when speaking. This is more common in rural areas, where visitors are still rare. In metropolitan areas, where people are familiar with foreign tourists, they're more open and less self-effacing. In tourist areas, as you'd expect, vendors have no hesitation in approaching you with their wares or taking you by the arm to try to convince you to buy something.

¡UPSIDE DOWN, RIGHT SIDE UP!

Many punctuation and spelling conventions used in Spanish have been adopted for use in written Quechua too. Questions *start* with an inverted question mark and end in a normal one; the same goes for exclamations ...!

FIRST ENCOUNTERS

ÑAWPAQ TUPANAKUY

You may find that people may not initiate conversations, or might wait to speak until they're sure that you've finished speaking – but don't hesitate to strike up a conversation, as people are very willing to talk to you once you've shown some interest.

How are you?

ee·mai·*nah*·lyahn kah·*shahn*·kee?   *¿Imaynallan kashanki?*

Fine. And you?

ah·lyee·*lyahn*·mee. kahn·*ree*?   *Allillanmi. ¿Qanrí?*

What's your name?

ee·mahn soo·*tee*·kee?   *¿Iman sutiyki?*

My name is ...

...n *soo*·tee   *...-n sutiy.*

I'd like to introduce you to ...

...·wahn rekh·see·nah·*kui*·chees   *...-wan riqsinakuychis.*

I'm pleased to meet you.

ahn·*chah*·tahn koo·see·*koo*·nee rekh·sees·*pai*·kee   *Anchatan kusikuni riqsispayki.*

MAKING CONVERSATION

IMALLAMANTAPAS RIMAY

Talking about the weather, local food and customs, or asking directions, are always safe openers. Personal questions about age, marital status, income and plans for the day are also perfectly acceptable in Quechua societies. If you're uncomfortable discussing such topics, steer the conversation in another direction, perhaps by answering with a little joke – 'I'm very old', *Sinchi machuñan kani*, *seen*·chee mah·*choo*·nyahn *kah*·nee, or 'I make enough money to travel once in a while', *Mayninpi purinallaypaqmi qulqita tarini*, mai·*neen*·pee poo·ree·nah·lyai·*pahkh*·mee kol·*ke*·tah tah·*ree*·nee.

Great day, isn't it?
  soo·mahkh *p'oon*·chai,
  ree·kee?

*Sumaq p'unchay,
¿riki?*

It's cold/hot today, isn't it?
  ahn·*chah*·tah chee·ree·shahn/
  roo·*p·hah*·shahn *ree*·kee?

*Anchata chirishan/
ruphashan, ¿riki?*

Are you waiting too?
  kahm·pees
  soo·yah·ree·shahn·*kee*·choo?

*¿Qampis
suyarishankichu?*

Where are you going?
  mai·*tah*·tahkh ree·*shahn*·kee?

¿Maytataq rishanki?

What are you doing?
  ee·mah·*tah*·tahkh
  ru·wah·*shahn*·kee?

*¿Imatataq
ruwashanki?*

What's this called?
  ee·*mah*·tahkh *kai*·pah
  soo·teen?

*¿Imataq kaypa
sutin?*

SAY CHEESE & THANK YOU

If you want to take pictures of indigenous people, ask their permission first. It would be considered rude not to offer some little thank-you gift afterwards. In fact, don't be surprised if you're asked outright for some cash!

Can I take a photo (of you)?
ah·*lyee*·choo p-hoo·*too*·tah
hor·koy·kee·*mahn*·choo?

¿*Allichu phututa*
hurquykimanchu?

Beautiful!
soo·mahkh!/ah·nyah·*nyow!*

¡*Sumaq!/¡Añañáw!*

What a beautiful village this is!
ee·ma *soo*·makh *lyakh*·ta!

¡*Ima sumaq llaqta!*

It's great here.
ahn·chah ah·*lyeen*·mee
kai·pee

Ancha allinmi
kaypi.

I'm here ...
    ...n *kai*·pee
    kah·*shah*·nee

    ...n *kaypi*
    kashani.

    for a holiday
    (vacation)
    how·kai
    pah·chah·*rai*·koo

    hawkay
    pacharayku

    on business
    lyahn·k'ah·nai·*rai*·koo

    llank'anayrayku

    to study
    yah·chah·nai·*rai*·koo

    yachanayrayku

How long are you here for?
  hai·k'ahkh·*kah*·mahn
  kai·pee *kahn*·kee?

¿Hayk'aqkaman
kaypi kanki?

I'm here for ... weeks/days.
  no·kah ... see·*mah*·nah/
  p'oon·chai kai·pee kah·sahkh

Nuqa ... simana/
p'unchay kaypi kasaq.

We're here for ... weeks/days.
  no·*kai*·koo ... see·*mah*·nah/
  p'oon·chai kai·pee
  kah·*sahkh*·koo

Nuqayku ... simana/
p'unchay kaypi
kasaqku.

NATIONALITIES

TUKUY RIKCH'AQ LLAQTAYUQKUNA

You'll find that many country names in Quechua are similar to English.

Where are you from?
  mai·*mahn*·tahn *kahn*·kee?

¿Maymantan kanki?

I'm from ...	*no*·kah ...·*mahn*·tah *kah*·nee	Nuqa ...-manta kani.
We're from ...	no·*kai*·koo ...·*mahn*·tah *kai*·koo	Nuqayku ...-manta kayku.
Australia	ows·*trah*·lyah	Awstraliya
Canada	kah·*nah*·dah	Kanada
England	een·lah·*tee*·rah	Inlatira
Europe	yoo·*roo*·pah	Yurupa
India	*een*·dyah	Indya
Ireland	eer·*lahn*·dah	Irlanda
Japan	*hah*·pun	Hapun
New Zealand	*nui*·wah	Nuywa
	see·*lahn*·dyah	Silandya
Scotland	ees·*koo*·syah	Iskusya
the USA	ees·*tah*·doos	Istadus
	oo·*nee*·dus	Unidus
Wales	*gah*·lees	Galis

I live in/by the/a ...	*no·kah ...·pee tee·yah·nee*	*Nuqa ...-pi tiyani.*
city	*lyahkh·tah*	*llaqta*
coast	*koos·tah*	*kusta*
countryside	*hah·wah·lyahkh·tah*	*hawallaqta*
mountains	*or·ko·koo·nah*	*urqukuna*
village	*lyahkh·tah*	*llaqta*

CULTURAL DIFFERENCES

SAPAQ YACHASQANCHISKUNA

Andeans are very generous, and if you express appreciation for something in someone's home, like a throw rug, a ceramic piece or some decoration, they might offer it to you as a gift. To avoid causing offence, gratefully accept the offer. The same is true for offers of food and drink.

If you're in a community during a celebration, people will make every effort to get you to participate, especially in activities such as dancing. It's not considered rude to resist such efforts, but be prepared for persistent attempts to involve you!

THE ANDEAN WAVE

If you want to beckon an Andean to you, hold your hand palm out, facing the other person, and waggle your fingers without moving the rest of your arm, as if you were waving goodbye to a child. If you wave your arm from side to side this will be understood as a goodbye gesture, as it generally is in Western cultures.

MEETING PEOPLE

How do you do this
in your country?

ee-mai·*nah*·tahkh
lyahkh·tai·*kee*·pee *kai*·tah
roo·wai·*kee*·chees?

*¿Imaynataq
llaqtaykipi kayta
ruwaykichis?*

Is this a local or national custom?

wah·keen
lyahkh·tah·*koo*·nahkh ee·chah
lyoo lyahkh·tah·*koo*·nahkh
kow·sai·neen·*koo*·choo chai?

*¿Wakin
llaqtakunaq icha
lliw llaqtakunaq
kawsayninkuchu chay?*

I'm sorry Sir/Madam,
it's not the custom in my country.

pahm·pah·chai·*koo*·wai
tai·*tail*/mah·*mai*, *mah*·nahn
lyahkh·*tai*·pah *chai*·tah
kow·sai·*neen*·choo

*Pampachaykuway
taytáy/mamáy, manan
llaqtaypa chayta
kawsayninchu.*

Please don't be offended.

ah·*lyee*·choo ah·mah
p-hee·nyah·*kui*·choo

*Allichu ama
phiñakuychu.*

I don't mind watching, but
I'd prefer not to participate.

k-hah·*wai*·tah
k-hah·wai·*mahn*·mee,
ee·*chah*·kah *mah*·nahn
chai·tah roo·*wai*·tah
moo·nai·*mahn*·choo

*Qhawayta
qhawaymanmi,
ichaqa manan
chayta ruwayta
munaymanchu.*

(But) I'll give it a go.

(ee·*chah*·kah)
ah·tee·pahs·kah·*lyai*·tah
roo·wai·*koo*·sahkh

*(Ichaqa)
atipasqallayta
ruwaykusaq.*

Let's dance!

too·*soo*·soon!

¡Tususun!

I don't know how to dance.

mah·nahn too·*sui*·tah
yah·chah·*nee*·choo

*Manan tusuyta
yachanichu.*

THANKS!

There are two ways to say thank you in Quechua, the traditional *'Sulpáy'*, sool·pai, and *'Añay'*, ah·nyai, which is increasingly popular these days.

local	kai lyahkh·*tah*·pee	*kay llaqta*
national	lyoo	*lliw*
	lyahkh·tah·koo·*nah*·pee	*llaqtakunapi*
everybody	*lyah*·pahn/lyah·*pahn*·koo	*llapan/llapanku*

AGE		**WATA**
How old are you, Sir/Ma'am? (to adult)	*hai*·k'ah wah·tah·*yokh*·mee kahn·kee, tai·*tai*/mah·*mai*?	¿Hayk'a watayuqmi kanki, taytáy/mamáy?
How old is your child? (to mother)	*hai*·k'ah wah·tah·*yokh*·mee wah·*wai*·kee?	¿Hayk'a watayuqmi wawayki?
How old are you? (to child)	*hai*·k'ah wah·tah·chah·*yokh*·mee kahn·kee?	¿Hayk'a watachayuqmi kanki?
I'm ... years old.	*no*·kah ... wah·tah·*yokh*·mee kah·nee	Nuqa ... watayuqmi kani.

(See Numbers & Amounts for your age, page 167.)

MEETING PEOPLE

OCCUPATIONS

RUWANAKUNA

What do you do?

ee·*mah*·peen lyahn·*k'ahn*·kee
kai·pee?

¿*Imapin llank'anki
kaypi?*

I'm a/an ...

no·kah ...·n/·mee *kah*·nee

Nuqa ...-n/-mi kani.

aide/assistant	yah·*nah*·pahkh/	*yanapaq/*
	yah·nah·*pah*·kokh	*yanapakuq*
artist	ahr·*tees*·tah	*artista*
businessperson	*rahm*·tekh/*k·hah*·tokh/	*rantiq/qhatuq/*
	teen·*dah*·yokh	*tindayuq*
carpenter	kahr·peen·*tee*·roo	*karpintiru*
chef	*wai*·k'okh/	*wayk'uq/*
	wai·k'oo·*pah*·kokh	*wayk'upakuq*
community leader	kah·*mah*·chekh	*kamachiq*
craftsperson	ahr·tee·*sah*·noo	*artisanu*
dancer	*too*·sokh	*tusuq*
doctor	*dook*·toor	*duktur*
driver	*choo*·feer	*chufir*
engineer	een·hee·*nyee*·roo	*inhiñiru*
farmer	*chahkh*·rah roo·nah	*chakra runa*
fisherman	*chahly*·wah *hah*·p'ekh	*challwa hap'iq*
fortune teller	*wah*·tokh	*watuq*
healer	*hahm*·pekh	*hampiq*
journalist	peer·yoo·*dees*·tah	*piryudista*
labourer	*lyahn*·k'akh	*llank'aq*
lawyer	*yoo*·yai kokh/	*yuyay quq/*
	ah·woo·*gah*·roo	*awugaru*
mayor	ahl·*kahl*·dee	*alkaldi*
mechanic	mee·kah·*nee*·koo	*mikaniku*
minister (pastor)	*roo*·nah mee·chekh	*runa michiq*
nurse	*on*·kokh	*unquq*
	yah·*nah*·pahkh	*yanapaq*
office worker	oo·fee·see·*nah*·pee	*ufisinapi*
	lyahn·k'akh	*llank'aq*

police officer	wahr·*dee*·yah	*wardiya*
priest	*tai*·tah koo·rah	*tayta kura*
scientist	hah·*mow*·t'ah	*hamawt'a*
shepherd	mee·chekh	*michiq*
singer	*tah*·kekh	*takiq*
student	yah·chai moo·nahkh	*yachay munaq*
teacher	yah·*chah*·chekh	*yachachiq*
university lecturer/ professor	hah·*mow*·t'ah	*hamawt'a*
waiter	mee·*k·hoo*·nah	*mikhuna*
	wah·*see*·pee	*wasipi*
	lyahn·k'ahkh	*llank'aq*
writer	*kel*·kahkh	*qilqaq*

I'm retired.
mah·*nah*·nyahn
lyahn·k'ah·*nee*·choo,
sah·mah·koo·*nee*·nyahn

*Manañan
llank'anichu,
samakuniñan.*

I'm unemployed.
mah·nah lyahn·k'ai·*nee*·yokh
kah·nee

*Mana llank'ayniyuq
kani.*

What are you studying?
ee·*mah*·tahkh
yah·chah·*shahn*·kee?

*¿Imatataq
yachashanki?*

I'm studying ...
no·kah ...·tahn
yah·chah·*shah*·nee

*Nuqa ...-tan
yachashani.*

art	*ahr*·tee	*arti*
arts/humanities	ee·mai·*mah*·nah yoo·yai·*koo*·nah	*imaymana yuyaykuna*
engineering	een·hee·nyee·*ree*·yah	*inhiñiriya*
English	*een*·lees	*inlis*
languages	ee·mai·*mah*·nah see·mee·*koo*·nah	*imaymana simikuna*
medicine	mee·dee·*see*·nah	*midisina*
science	hah·*moo*·t'ai	*hamut'ay*
Spanish	kahs·tee·*lyah*·noo	*kastillanu*

MEETING PEOPLE

FEELINGS   SINTIMINTUKUNA

If someone asks, 'How are you?', your first response should be a generic 'I'm well' or 'I'm not well'.

How are you?
ee·mai·*nah*·lyahn kah·*shahn*·kee?   *¿Imaynallan kashanki?*
I'm well.
ah·*lyeen*·lyahn kah·*shah*·nee   *Allinllan kashani.*
I'm not so good.
mah·nahn ah·*lyeen*·choo   *Manan allinchu*
kah·*shah*·nee   *kashani.*

Are you ...?	....choo kah·*shahn*·kee?	*¿...-chu kashanki?*
I'm ...	....n kah·*shah*·nee	*...-n kashani.*
afraid	mahn·*chahs*·kah	*manchasqa*
angry	fee·*nyahs*·kah	*phiñasqa*
depressed	pee·see·*chahs*·kah	*pisichasqa*
grateful	son·kon·chah·*koos*·kah	*sunqunchakusqa*
happy	koo·*sees*·kah	*kusisqa*
in a hurry	ah·poo·*rahs*·kah	*apurasqa*
inspired	kahly·pah·chah·*koos*·kah	*kallpachakusqa*
sad	lyah·*kees*·kah	*llakisqa*
tired	sai·*k'oos*·kah	*sayk'usqa*
worried	lyah·*kees*·kah	*llakisqa*

A phrase such as 'I'm afraid' is easy enough to translate from English to Quechua, but 'I'm cold' is more problematic. These feelings require special phrases to express them:

I'm cold.
chee·ree·wah·*shahn*·mee   *Chiriwashanmi.*
I'm hot.
roo·p·hah·ree·wah·   *Ruphariwa-*
shahn·mee   *shanmi.*
I'm hungry.
yahr·kah·wah·*shahn*·mee   *Yarqawashanmi.*

I'm thirsty.
    ch'ah·kee·wah·*shahn*·mee   *Ch'akiwashanmi.*
I'm sleepy.
    poo·*nyui*·mee   *Puñuymi*
    ai·sah·*wah*·shahn   *aysawashan.*
I'm right. (correct)
    rah·soon·nee·*yokh*·mee   *Rasunniyuqmi*
    kah·nee   *kani.*
I'm sorry. (condolence)
    ahn·*chah*·tahn   *Anchatan*
    lyah·kee·*pai*·kee   *llakipayki.*

BREAKING THE LANGUAGE BARRIER

RIMANAKUYTA ATIY

Do you speak ...?   ... ree·mahn·*kee*·choo?   *¿... rimankichu?*
    English   een·*lees*·tah   *inlista*
    Quechua   roo·nah·see·*mee*·tah   *runasimita*
    Spanish   kahs·tee·lyah·*noo*·tah   *kastillanuta*

Yes, I do.
    ah·*ree,* ree·*mah*·neen   *Arí, rimanin.*
No, I don't.
    mah·nahn, ree·mah·*nee*·choo   *Manan, rimanichu.*
I speak a little bit.
    no·kah pee·see·*lyah*·tah   *Nuqa pisillata*
    ree·*mah*·nee   *rimani.*
Who speaks English here?
    pee·tahkh *kai*·pee   *¿Pitaq kaypi*
    een·*lees*·tah *ree*·mahn?   *inlista riman?*

Do you understand?
    een·teen·deen·*kee*·choo?   *¿Intindinkichu?*

I (don't) understand.
    (mah·nahn)   *(Manan)*
    een·teen·dee·*nee*·choo   *intindinichu.*

Could you speak more slowly?
    ah·lyee·lyah·*mahn*·tah   *¿Allillamanta*
    ree·mai·koon·kee·*mahn*·choo?   *rimaykunkimanchu?*

Could you repeat that?
    yah·pah·*mahn*·tah *chai*·tah   *¿Yapamanta chayta*
    ree·mai·koon·kee·*mahn*·choo?   *rimaykunkimanchu?*

Please write it down.
    ah·*lyee*·choo *kel*·kai   *Allichu qilqay.*

How do you say this in Quechua?
(when pointing to something)
    ee·mah·neen·*chees*·mee   *¿Imaninchismi*
    kai·tah roo·nah·see·*mee*·pee?   *kayta runasimipi?*

What does ... mean?
    ee·mah nee·nahn·*chees*·mee ...?   *¿Ima ninanchismi ...?*

RELIGION   RILIHIYUN

Religion is a topic of everyday conversation – it's certainly not
a taboo subject. While the Andean countries are officially
Catholic, there's actually a fair amount of freedom of religion.
All of the Christian religions are represented, as well as
many Eastern religions and beliefs. Names of religions were
simply borrowed from Spanish and adapted to the Quechua
pronunciation system.

What's your religion?
    ee·*mah*·tahkh   *¿Imataq*
    ree·lee·hee·yun·*nee*·kee?   *rilihiyunniyki?*

I'm (a/an) ...   *no*·kah ....n/·mee   *Nuqa* ...-n/-mi
                      kah·nee   *kani.*

Adventist	ahd·ween·*tees*·tah	*adwintista*
Baptist	wow·*tees*·tah	*wawtista*
Buddhist	woo·*dees*·tah	*wudista*
Christian	krees·tee·*yah*·noo	*kristiyanu*
Evangelist	ee·wahn·hee·*lees*·tah	*iwanhilista*
Hindu	*een*·doo	*indu*
Jehovah's Witness	ee·wahn·hee·*lees*·tah	*iwanhilista*
Jewish	hoo·*dee*·yoo	*hudiyu*
Lutheran	loo·tee·*rah*·noo	*lutiranu*
Methodist	mee·too·*dees*·tah	*mitudista*
Mormon	*moor*·moon	*murmun*
Muslim	moo·*sool*·mahn	*musulman*
Protestant	proo·tees·*tahn*·tee	*prutistanti*

I'm not religious.
mah·nah   *Mana*
ree·lee·hee·yoon·nee·*yokh*·mee   *rilihiyunniyuqmi*
kah·nee   *kani.*

IT'S THE END OF THE WORD

When using -n/-mi, choose the -n ending when the preceding root word ends in a vowel, and the -mi ending when it ends in a consonant: eg, *adwintista*-n, ahd·ween·*tees*·tah, or *murmun-mi*, moor·*moon*·mee. Note that using the -mi ending will change which syllable is stressed.

MEETING PEOPLE

COSMOVISION & CATHOLICISM

Catholicism as practised by the indigenous people in the Andes has some intriguing differences from Western Catholicism.

The Andean religion, before the conquistadors introduced Christianity, was more a cosmovision than simply a religion – it was an entire way of viewing the world and explaining natural events. It was animistic, believing that animals and other elements of the natural world have souls. The highest deity was 'Father Sun', *Tayta Inti*, *tai·tah een·tee*, from whom the Incas believed themselves to be directly descended.

Obviously the Incas had great respect for the natural world and its power. Their sacred objects, or *wak'as*, *wah·k'ahs*, were mountain peaks, rivers and lakes, all of whose souls needed to be appeased regularly with ritual offerings, usually of food or drink. *Pachamama*, *pah·chah·mah·mah*, was 'Mother Earth', the nurturing protector and life-giver of all beings, and it was particularly important to pay her for her bounty. This was done through a major celebration that took place every August, known as 'payment to Mother Earth' or *haywakuy*, *hai·wah·kui*. Payments consisted of offerings of coca leaves, food or beverages.

When the Spaniards arrived (1532), they began to convert the locals to Catholicism. The Andeans seemed to accept the teaching of the missionaries fairly readily but, in reality, they did not reject their previous beliefs to accept the new ones. Rather, they syncretised them, or layered

COSMOVISION & CATHOLICISM

them on top of their existing beliefs. The Christian belief in heaven and hell led them to add similar spiritual territories to their organisational schema of the world. In addition to *kay pacha*, kai *pah·*chah, the world in which people dwell, there is *hanaq pacha*, *hah·*nahkh *pah·*chah, the world above, where the gods dwell, and *ukhu pacha*, *oo·*k-hoo *pah·*chah, the world below, a world of shadows and darkness. In the Andean cosmology, these three worlds interconnect and their inhabitants interact.

Another example of this syncretism is the Andean belief in God and active worship of the saints. They consider Jesus and the Virgin Mary to belong to this category of saints. Interestingly, they have blended the identities of the Catholic saints with their own *apus*, *ah·*poos, 'principal mountain gods' and *wak'as*, *wah·*k'ahs, 'sacred places'. This was a logical thing to do. For Western Catholics, the saints serve as intermediaries between humans and their God, and in the ancient Andean cosmovision, the *apus* and *wak'as* also served an intermediary function. The Virgin Mary herself came to be associated with *Pachamama*, the Earth Mother, the greatest of all female deities.

The most obvious manifestation of this practice is the habit of putting crosses on mountain tops, and holding traditional festivals on Catholic saints' days, so that the 'Spanish' God and saints and the traditional mountain *apus* and *wak'as* can be worshipped at the same time.

I'm Catholic, but I don't
go to mass.
    kah·too·*lee*·koon *kah*·nee,
    mah·*nah*·tahkh
    mee·*sah*·mahn ree·*nee*·choo

Katulikun kani,
manataq
misaman rinichu.

I believe in God.
    tai·tah dee·yoos·*mahn*·mee
    ee·*nyee*·nee

Tayta Diyusmanmi
iñini.

I'm interested in astrology.
    koy·lyoor·koo·nah·*mahn*·tah
    yah·*chai*·tah moo·*nah*·nee

Quyllurkunamanta
yachayta munani.

I'm interested in philosophy.
    hah·moo·t'ai·*mahn*·tah
    yah·*chai*·tah moo·*nah*·nee

Hamut'aymanta
yachayta munani.

I'm an atheist.
    mah·nahn dee·*yoos*·mahn
    ee·nyee·*nee*·choo

Manan Diyusman
iñinichu.

Can I attend this service/mass?
    kai kool·*too*·tah/mee·*sah*·tah
    oo·yah·ree·*mahn*·choo?

¿Kay kultuta/misata
uyarimanchu?

Can I pray here?
    mah·nyah·kui·*mahn*·choo
    kai·pee?

¿Mañakuymanchu
kaypi?

Where can I pray/worship?
    mai·*pee*·tahkh
    yoo·pai·*chai*·mahn?

¿Maypitaq
yupaychayman?

Is there a church here?
    kahn·choo een·*lee*·sah *kai*·pee?

¿Kanchu inlisa kaypi?

ancestor	*nyow*·pah *ai*·lyoo	ñawpa ayllu
baptism	oo·*lee*·yai	uliyay
christening	wow·*tee*·sai	wawtisay
church	een·*lee*·sah;	inlisa;
	dee·*yoos*·pah *wah*·seen	Diyuspa wasin
cross	*koo*·roos	kurus
deity	*dee*·yoos *kai*·neen	Diyus kaynin
devil	*sahkh*·rah/*soo*·pai	saqra/supay
evil spirit	*so*·k'ah	suq'a
Father Sun	*tai*·tah *een*·tee	Tayta Inti
Festival of the Sun	*een*·tee *rai*·mee	Inti Raymi
God	*dee*·yoos/*yah*·yah	Diyus/Yaya
creator of the Earth	pah·chah·*kah*·mahkh	Pachakamaq
creator of the Incas	wee·rah·*ko*·chah	Wiraqucha
mountain god	*ah*·poo	Apu
secondary mountain gods	*ow*·kee	awki
Incan priest	*oo*·moo	umu
lake	*mah*·mah *ko*·chah	Mama Qucha
lightning	ee·*lyah*·pah	illapa
mass	*mee*·sah	misa
Mother Earth	pah·chah·*mah*·mah	Pachamama
Mother Moon	*mah*·mah *kee*·lyah	Mama Killa
to pray	mah·*nyah*·kui	mañakuy
prayer	mah·*nyah*·kokh	mañakuq
priest	*tai*·tah *koo*·rah; *yah*·yah	tayta kura; yaya
procession	proo·*see*·yoon	prusiyun
river	*mah*·yoo	mayu
sabbath	yoo·pai·*chah*·nah	yupaychana
	poon·ch'ai	punch'ay
sacred place	*wah*·k'ah	wak'a
sacrifice	*hai*·wai	hayway

saint (m/f)	tai·*tah*·chah/	*taytacha/*
	mah·*mah*·chah	*mamacha*
shrine	kah·*pee*·lyah	*kapilla*
sin	*hoo*·chah	*hucha*
to sin	hoo·chah·*lyee*·kui	*huchallikuy*
stars	koy·lyoor·*koo*·nah	*quyllurkuna*
temple	*mahn*·ko *wah*·see	*manqu wasi*
Temple of the Sun	ko·ree·*kahn*·chah	*Qurikancha*
thunder	*k-hahkh*·yah	*qhaqya*
witch	*lai*·kah	*layqa*

GETTING AROUND

Arranging journeys by plane, train, bus or taxi is generally done in Spanish or English in the Andean region. In Quechua-speaking communities, such forms of transport are not common – even street signs are usually in Spanish.

Nevertheless, Quechua will be the key to seeking your own way in remote areas, if you need to ask whether a car or bus is available, or which way you should go.

FINDING YOUR WAY
MAYTAPAS RIYTA YACHAY

Excuse me Sir/Madam ...
pahm·pah·chah·*yoo*·wai   *Pampachayuway*
tai·tai/mah·*mai* ...   *tayta/mamay ...*

Where am I?
mai·peen kah·*shah*·nee?   *¿Maypin kashani?*

I'm looking for ...
...·tahn mahs·k·hah·*shah*·nee   *...-tan maskhashani.*

Where's the ...?   mai·*pee*·tahkh ...?   *¿Maypitaq ...?*
   bus station   oo·*nee*·woos *sah*·yahn   *uniwus sayan*
   dock/pier   *wahm*·poo *sah*·yahn   *wampu sayan*
   road to ...   ...·tah ree·*nah*·pahkh   *...-ta rinapaq*
         nyahn   *ñan*
   train station   treen *sah*·yahn   *trin sayan*

LOCAL TRANSPORT

If you're adventurous, try riding in the back of a pickup truck to get from one place to another. This may be the only way to get off the beaten track. You're exposed to the elements, but it's a great way to see the countryside and get to know the locals. You're expected to offer some sort of payment to the driver, as the Andeans do themselves.

GETTING AROUND

What time does the ... leave?	ee·mah oo·*rah*·tahkh ... *lyokh*·seen?	¿Ima urataq ... lluqsin?
What time does the ... arrive?	ee·mah oo·*rahs*·mee ... chah·*yah*·moon?	¿Ima urasmi ... chayamun?
boat	*wahm*·poo	wampu
bus	oo·*nee*·woos	uniwus
minibus	oo·nee·*woos*·chah/ *meek*·roo	uniwuscha/ mikru
train	treen	trin

How do we get to ...?
ee·mai·*nah*·tahkh ....man
chah·*yahn*·chees?
¿Imaynataq ...-man chayanchis?

Is it close by?
sees·*pah*·choo?
¿Sispachu?

Can we walk there?
chah·kee·*lyah*·wahn
ree·koo·*mahn*·choo *chai*·mahn?
¿Chakillawan riykumanchu chayman?

Can you show me (on the map)?
(mah·*pah*·pee)
k·hah·wai·kah·chee·
wahn·kee·*mahn*·choo?
(Mapapi) ¿Qhawaykachi- wankimanchu?

BUT HOW WILL IT END?

Remember, when adding suffixes to words, choose the *first* ending when the root word ends in a vowel, and the *second* ending when it ends in a consonant.

What's the name of this ...?	ee·*mah*·tahkh kai ...kh/·pah *soo*·teen?	¿Imataq kay ...-q/-pa sutin?
city/village	*lyahkh*·tah	llaqta
highway	*pees*·tah	pista
path	nyahn	ñan
road	kah·ree·*tee*·rah	karitira
street	*kah*·lyee	kalli

DIRECTIONS

Straight ahead.
  syookh/dee·*ree*·choo
To the left/right.
  lyoo·*k'ee*·mahn/pah·*nyah*·mahn
Turn at the next corner/street.
  hah·mokh k'oo·*choo*·pee/
  kah·*lyee*·pee moo·*yui*·kui

YACHACHIYKUNA

Siwk/Dirichu.

Lluq'iman/Pañaman.

Hamuq k'uchupi/
kallipi muyuykuy.

across (from)	cheem·*pah*·pee	*chimpapi*
behind	k-*he*·pah	*qhipa*
far	*kah*·roo	*karu*
here	*kai*·pee	*kaypi*
in front (of)	nyow·*pahkh*·pee	*ñawpaqpi*
near	*sees*·pah	*sispa*
there	*chai*·pee/chai·*nekh*·pee/	*chaypi/chayniqpi/*
	hah·*kai*·pee	*haqaypi*

GETTING AROUND

north	*wee*·chai	*wichay*
south	*oo*·rai	*uray*
east	*een*·tekh lyokh·*see*·nahn	*intiq lluqsinan*
west	*een*·tekh cheen·*kah*·nahn	*intiq chinkanan*

Thank you for showing us the way.

sool·*pai nyahn*·tah
rekh·see·chee·*moo*·wahs
kai·kee·koo·*mahn*·tah

Sulpáy ñanta
riqsichimuwa-
sqaykikumanta.

For more instructions, see Taxi, below.

ADDRESSES   DIRIKSIYUNKUNA

Addresses are generally indicated in Spanish rather than in
Quechua. A typical address might look like this:

> Sra. María Condori Guzmán
> Avenida Tullomayo 428
> Cuzco, Peru

Large cities, such as Lima, La Paz and Quito, may have several
postal codes, but this is not common. Post office boxes *(apartado*
or *casilla* in Spanish) are popular too:

> Sr. José Huamán Mamani
> Apartado Postal 477 (or Casilla Postal 477)
> Cochabamba, Bolivia

TAXI   TAKSI

Taxis are not widely available in the more rural Quechua-
speaking areas. To hold a licence, the driver must speak Spanish,
so arrangements are generally made in Spanish – or possibly in
English in larger cities.

There are two kinds of taxis. A *taxi oficial* is a state-regulated
taxi, which is more likely (but not guaranteed) to have a meter;
a *taxi particular* is an informal, privately owned taxi – fares are
negotiable. You can flag down either sort in large cities.

Make sure you bargain and settle on a price to your destination before getting in. Taxis are generally inexpensive, but some drivers will raise their prices when dealing with a foreigner. See Bargaining, page 127, for more on this.

Sir/Madam, I want to go to ...
tai·*tail*/mah·*mai* ...·tah
ree·tah moo·*nah*·nee

Taytáy/Mamáy ...-ta riyta munani.

How much is it to go to ...?
hai·k'ahn *kwees*·tahn ...·tah ree·*nah*·pahkh?

¿Hayk'an kwistan ...-ta rinapaq?

How much is the ticket/fare?
hai·k'ahn *kwees*·tahn pah·*sah*·hee?

¿Hayk'an kwistan pasahi?

Instructions

Yachachiykuna

Please take me to ...
ah·*lyee*·choo ...·tah ah·*pah*·wai

Allichu ...-ta apaway.

Keep going straight!
syookh!

¡Siwk!

The next street to the left/right.
hah·mokh kah·*lyee*·pee
pah·*nyah*·mahn/lyo·*k'e*·mahn
moo·*yui*·kui

Hamuq kallipi pañaman/lluq'iman muyuykuy.

Please slow down.
ah·*lyee*·choo
ah·*lyee*·lyah·*mahn*·tah ree

Allichu allillamanta riy.

Please wait here.
ah·*lyee*·choo *kai*·pee *soo*·yai

Allichu kaypi suyay.

Stop here!
sah·yai *kai*·pee!

¡Sayay kaypi!

Stop at the corner!
chai k'hoo·*choo*·pee *sah*·yai!

¡Chay k'uchupi sayay!

GETTING AROUND

BUYING TICKETS   WULITUKUNATA RANTIY

Haggling is common when buying tickets for travel. You can even bargain with a travel agent, but purchasing directly from a bus or train station means paying the posted price. Foreigners will often pay more than locals do, especially in tourist areas. See Bargaining, page 127, for more on this.

Buying tickets at bus stations is usually done in Spanish. Flight arrangements are always made in Spanish or in English.

Where can I buy a ticket?
mai·*pee*·tahkh
woo·lee·*too*·tah
rahn·tee·*rui*·mahn?

¿Maypitaq
wulituta
rantirquyman?

How much is the ticket/fare?
hai·k'ahn *kwees*·tahn
pah·*sah*·hee?

¿Hayk'an kwistan
pasahi?

How long does it take to get to ...?
hai·k'ah oo·rah·*pee*·tahkh
...·mahn chah·*yahn*·chees?

¿Hayk'a urapitaq
...-man chayanchis?

BUS & CAR   UNIWUS, KARRU

Bus services come in a wide range of quality and service levels, and once again, transactions are conducted almost exclusively in Spanish. However, you might want to inform yourself on local bus services – or the availability of a car where there are no buses – by asking local Quechua speakers.

What time does the ... bus arrive?	ee·mah oo·*rah*·tahkh ... oo·nee·*woos*·kah chah·*yah*·moon?	¿Ima urataq ... uniwusqa chayamun?
What time does the ... car leave?	ee·mah oo·*rah*·tahkh ... kah·*rroo*·kah *lyok*·seen?	¿Ima urataq ... karruqa lluqsin?
first	*nyow*·pahkh	ñawpaq
last	*k·he*·pah	qhipa
next	*hah*·mokh	hamuq

GOING MY WAY?

In rural areas where there's little or no public transport available, cars often double as buses. Drivers will be on the lookout for anyone going in the same direction. You'll need to agree on a price before accepting the lift – see Taxi and Buying Tickets (pages 68, 70).

Does this bus/car go to ...?
  kai oo·*nee*·woos/*kah*·rroo
  ...·mahn *reen*·choo?
How many times a day
do buses/cars pass by here?
  hai·k'ah *koo*·teen
  oo·nee·woos·*koo*·nah/
  kah·rroo·*koo*·nah *kai*·pee
  pah·sahn *sah*·pah p'oon·chai?
Where does this bus/car go?
  mai·tahn/*mai*·*mahn*·mee
  kai oo·*nee*·woos/*kah*·rroo reen?
Where's the bus/car stop?
  mai·*pee*·tahkh oo·*nee*·woos/
  kah·rroo *sah*·yahn?
Which bus/car goes to ...?
  mai·ken oo·*nee*·*woos*·tahkh/
  kah·*rroo*·tahkh ...·mahn reen?
Where can I catch the bus/car to ...?
  mai·*pee*·tahkh ...·mahn
  ree·*nai*·pahkh oo·nee·*woos*·tah/
  kah·*rroo*·tah hah·p'ee·*rui*·mahn?
This is my seat.
  tee·yah·*nai*·mee *kai*·kah

*¿Kay uniwus/karru
...·man rinchu?*

*¿Hayk'a kutin
uniwuskuna/
karrukuna kaypi
pasan sapa p'unchay?*

*¿Maytan/maymanmi
kay uniwus/karru rin?*

*¿Maypitaq uniwus/
karru sayan?*

*¿Mayqin uniwustaq/
karrutaq ...·man rin?*

*¿Maypitaq ...·man
rinaypaq uniwusta/
karruta hap'irquyman?*

Tiyanaymi kayqa.

GETTING AROUND

Could you let me know
when we get to ...?
    ah·*lyee*·choo ...·mahn   ¿Allichu ...-man
    chah·yahkh·*teen*·chees   chayaqtinchis
    wee·lyai·koo·wahn·   willaykuwan-
    kee·*mahn*·choo?   kimanchu?

Can you tell the driver to stop?
    ah·*lyee*·choo *sah*·yai   ¿Allichu sayay
    neen·kee·*mahn*·choo   ninkimanchu
    choo·feer·*tah*·kah?   chuphirtaqa?

I'd like to get off here.
    kai·pee oo·rai·*kui*·tahn   Kaypi uraykuytan
    moo·*nah*·nee   munani.

THE FUN BUS

When travelling on local buses and minibuses, be
prepared for an extraordinary acoustic treat and
flexible ideas on what constitutes safe driving. Between
passengers yelling at the conductor, the conductor yelling
out the stops as they come up, and the driver yelling
out the window at other drivers, things can get loud.
There may be music blasting out through numerous
speakers. Local performers might climb on to give an
impromptu performance complete with expectations of
tips, while local vendors tout their wares. Buses are often
overcrowded, especially when animals and food products
are on board.

TRAIN   TRIN

Trains don't run nearly as frequently as buses, but they're generally more comfortable for long-distance travel.

What's the name of this station?
ee·*mah*·tahkh kai   ¿*Imataq kay*
sah·*yah*·nahkh *soo*·teen?   *sayanaq sutin?*

What's the name of the next station?
ee·*mah*·tahkh *hah*·mokh   ¿*Imataq hamuq*
sah·*yah*·nahkh *soo*·teen?   *sayanaq sutin?*

Does this train stop at (Arequipa)?
(ah·ree·kee·*pah*·pee)   ¿(*Arikipapi*)
sah·*yahn*·choo kai *treen*·kah?   *sayanchu kay trinqa?*

There's no train today.
mah·nan treen *kahn*·choo   *Manan trin kanchu*
koo·nahn *p'oon*·chai   *kunan p'unchay.*

Can I sit here?
tee·yai·*mahn*·choo *kai*·pee?   ¿*Tiyaymanchu kaypi?*

I want to get off at ...
...·pee oo·rai·*kui*·tah   ...-*pi uraykuyta*
moo·*nah*·nee   *munani.*

BOAT   WAMPU

Boat travel in the Andes might be by canoe for travelling along rivers and other waterways, or by motor boat or hovercraft when travelling from island to island on large lakes such as Titicaca. Even luxury cruise ships, *hatun wampu*, hah·toon *wahm*·poo, are an option, for those wanting to visit the Galapagos Islands.

Arrangements for this type of transport are usually made through travel agencies, although you may also be able to negotiate on the spot.

Where can I find a boat that
goes to ...?
mai·*pee*·tahkh wahm·*poo*·tah   ¿*Maypitaq wamputa*
tah·ree·*rui*·mahn ...·tah   *tarirquyman ...-ta*
ree·*nai*·pahkh?   *rinaypaq?*

GETTING AROUND

Where does that boat go?
mai·*tah*·tahkh/mai·*mahn*·tahkh
chai *wahm*·poo reen?

¿*Maytataq/Maymantaq
chay wampu rin?*

Where does the boat leave from?
mai·mahn·*tah*·tahkh
wahm·poo *lyokh*·seen?

¿*Maymantaq
wampu lluqsin?*

What time does the boat arrive/leave?
ee·mah oo·*rahs*·mee *wahm*·poo
chah·*yah*·moon/*lyokh*·seen?

¿*Ima urasmi wampu
chayamun/lluqsin?*

DRIVING   KARRU

Car rentals are generally only available in major cities. If you
decide to rent a car, services – from filling up to repairs – will be
handled in Spanish.

In the larger cities and tourist areas, motorcycling is also
possible. Organised tours are the easiest, but renting or buying
your own motorcycle is an option.

Is there a mechanic around here?
kahn·choo mee·kah·*nee*·koo
kai·pee?

¿*Kanchu mikaniku
kaypi?*

Is there a gas/petrol station nearby?
gree·foo *kahn*·choo kai·pee?

¿*Griphu kanchu kaypi?*

Where can I buy gas/petrol?
mai·peen gah·soo·lee·*nah*·tah
rahn·tee·*rui*·mahn?

¿*Maypin gasulinata
rantirquyman?*

Does this road/highway/path
lead to ...?
kai kah·ree·*tee*·rah/*pees*·tah/nyahn
...·*mahn*·choo reen?

¿*Kay karitira/pista/ñan
...-manchu rin?*

How can I go to ...?
ee·*mai*·nahn ...·mahn
ree·mahn?

¿*Imaynan ...-man
riyman?*

Which is the way to ...?
mai·*neen*·tahn ...·mahn reen?

¿*Maynintan ...-man rin*

I'm lost.
cheen·kai cheen·*kai*·lyah
poo·ree·*koo*·nee

*Chinkay chinkaylla
purikuni.*

My car has broken down.
    kah·*rrui*·kah *mah*·nahn
    poo·*ree*·tah ah·*teen*·choo

*Karruyqa manan
puriyta atinchu.*

Is there a car here going to ...?
    kah·rroo *kahn*·choo *kai*·pee
    ...·mahn ree·*nah*·pahkh?

*¿Karru kanchu kaypi
...-man rinapaq?*

Where are you going?
    mai·tahn ree·*shahn*·kee?

¿Maytan rishanki?

I'm going to ...
    ...·tahn ree·*shah*·nee

...-tan rishani.

Can you take me there in your car?
    pahkh·tah kah·rrui·*kee*·pee
    ah·pah·wahn·*kee*·mahn
    chai·mahn?

*¿Paqta karruykipi
apawankiman
chayman?*

How much do I owe you?
    hai·k'ah·*tah*·tahkh
    mah·noo·*kui*·kee?

*¿Hayk'atataq
manukuyki?*

BICYCLE   WISIKILITA

Mountain biking is, for obvious reasons, one of the most popular forms of cycling in the Andes. Bicycles are available to rent or buy in larger cities and tourist areas.

Is ... within cycling distance?
    wee·see·kee·lee·*tah*·wahn
    ree·rui·*mahn*·choo ...·mahn?

*¿Wisikilitawan
rirquymanchu ...-man?*

Is there a bike path?
    kahm·choo wee·see·kee·*lee*·tah
    nyahn?

*¿Kanchu wisikilita
ñan?*

GETTING AROUND

Who can show me the bicycle paths?
pee·tahkh wee·see·kee·lee·tah
nyahn·koo·nah·tah
rekh·see·chee·wahn·mahn?

¿Pitaq wisikilita
ñankunata
riqsichiwanman?

Where can I hire a bicycle?
mai·pee·tahkh
wee·see·kee·lee·tah·tah
ahl·kee·lai·rui·man?

¿Maypitaq
wisikilitata
alkilarquyman?

How much is it per hour/day?
hai·k'ah·tahkh kwees·tahn
sah·pah oo·rah/p'oon·chai?

¿Hayk'ataq kwistan
sapa ura/p'unchay?

Where can I buy a bike?
mai·pee·tahkh
wee·see·kee·lee·tah·tah
rahn·tee·rui·mahn?

¿Maypitaq
wisikilitata
rantirquyman?

I have a flat tyre.
wee·see·kee·lee·tai·pah
lyahn·tahn·mee t'o·ko·ron

Wisikilitaypa llantanmi
t'uqurqun.

Could you help me please?
ah·lyee·choo
yah·nah·pah·yoo·wahn·
kee·mahn·choo?

¿Allichu
yanapayuwa-
nkimanchu?

bicycle	wee·see·kee·lee·tah	*wisikilita*
puncture	t'o·ko	*t'uqu*
seat	tee·yah·nah	*tiyana*
tyre(s)	lyahn·tah(koo·nah)	*llanta(kuna)*

QURPACHANA
ACCOMMODATION

Accommodation choices range from luxury hotels in the larger cities and popular tourist towns, to a humble sleeping space with a rural Andean family. In the smaller communities, a few words of Quechua might be the secret to a comfortable night's sleep.

FINDING ACCOMMODATION

QURPACHANATA MASKHAY

I'm looking for (a) ...	...·tah mahs·k-hah·*shah*·nee	...·ta *maskhashani.*
accommodation	*kor*·pah·*chah*·nah	*qurpachana*
camping ground	*kahr*·pah	*karpa*
	roo·wah·*nah*·pahkh	*ruwanapaq*
	pahm·pah	*pampa*
boarding house/ hotel	*kor*·pah *wah*·see	*qurpa wasi*
Where's a/the ... hotel?	mai·*pee*·tahkh ... *kor*·pah *wah*·see kahn?	*¿Maypitaq* ... *qurpa wasi kan?*
best	lyoo·*mahn*·tah *ahn*·chah *soo*·mahkh	*lliwmanta ancha sumaq*
cheap	*mah*·nah chah·*nee*·yohkh	*mana chaniyuq*
cheapest	lyoo·*mahn*·tah *pee*·see chah·*nee*·yokh	*lliwmanta pisi chaniyuq*
clean	pee·*chahs*·kah	*pichasqa*
good	*ah*·lyeen	*allin*

ACCOMMODATION

Is there a hotel here?
kahn·choo kor·pah
wah·see kai·pee?

¿Kanchu qurpa
wasi kaypi?

Is that a good hotel?
ah·lyeen kor·pah
wah·see·choo chai·kah?

¿Allin qurpa
wasichu chayqa?

Is that a clean hotel?
lui·loo·choo chai kor·pah
wah·see·kah?

¿Luyluchu chay qurpa
wasiqa?

Is that hotel nearby/far?
sees·pah·lyah·pee·choo/
kah·roo·pee·choo kah·shahn
chai kor·pah wah·see·kah?

¿Sispallapichu/
Karupichu kashan
chay qurpa wasiqa?

Could you show me
that hotel, please?
rekh·see·chee·wahn·kee·
mahn·choo chai kor·pah
wah·see·tah·kah?

¿Riqsichiwanki-
manchu chay qurpa
wasitaqa?

REQUESTS & QUERIES

MAÑAKUYKUNAPAS TAPUYKUNAPAS

Where can I sleep?
mai·pee·tahkh poo·nyoo·man?

¿Maypitaq puñuyman?

Is there a toilet here?
kahn·choo hees·p'ah·koo·nah/
ees·koo·sah·roo kai·pee?

¿Kanchu hisp'akuna/
iskusaru kaypi?

Where can I take a bath?
mai·pee·tahkh
ahr·mah·kui·mahn?

¿Maypitaq
armakuyman?

WATER ...

There are two different words for 'water': *unu*,
oo·noo, and *yaku*, *yah·koo*. The latter is used
throughout the Andes.

Is there water to wash myself?
   kahm·choo *oo*·noo/*yah*·koo
   mahkh·ch·hee·koo·*nai*·pahkh?
                    ¿Kanchu unu/yaku
                    maqchhikunaypaq?

Is there water to wash my face?
   kahm·choo *oo*·noo/*yah*·koo
   oo·p·hah·koo·*nai*·pahkh?
                    ¿Kanchu unu/yaku
                    uphakunaypaq?

Could you please heat up
some water for me?
   ah·*lyee*·choo oo·*noo*·tah/
   yah·*koo*·tah
   k'o·nyee·chee·poo·wahn-
   kee·*mahn*·choo?
                    ¿Allichu unuta/
                    yakuta
                    q'uñichipuwa-
                    nkimanchu?

Where can I wash my clothes?
   mai·*pee*·tahkh
   p'ah·chai·koo·*nah*·tah
   t'ahkh·sah·*rui*·mahn?
                    ¿Maypitaq
                    p'achaykunata
                    t'aqsarquyman?

Where's the river/spring?
   mai·*pee*·tahkh *mah*·yoo/
   pookh·yoo kahn?
                    ¿Maypitaq mayu/
                    pukyu kan?

Where can I find drinking water?
   mai·*pee*·tahkh ook·*yah*·nah
   oo·*noo*·tah tah·ree·*rui*·mahn?
                    ¿Maypitaq ukyana
                    unuta tarirquyman?

Is there clean water here?
   kahm·choo *ch'oo*·yah *oo*·noo/
   yah·koo *kai*·pee?
                    ¿Kanchu ch'uya unu/
                    yaku kaypi?

ACCOMMODATION

AROUND THE HOME

Remember that Andean houses may not have the luxury of running water or indoor toilets. Be sure to bring all of your own toiletries, and simply ask for a tub for washing.

At meal times, your host family will expect you to share in their food and conversation, and to try the different dishes on offer.

That was delicious!
   soo·mahkh mee·*k*·hoo·nah!   *¡Sumaq mikhuna!*

ACCOMMODATION

Is there anything to drink?
kahn·choo oo·kyah·*nah*·pahkh
ee·mah·*lyah*·pahs?

¿Kanchu ukyanapaq
imallapas?

May I have some herbal tea?
pahkh·tah *ko*·rah
oo·*noo*·tah/yah·*koo*·tah
ko·wahn·*kee*·mahn?

¿Paqta qura
unuta/yakuta
quwankiman?

Is there anything to eat?
kahn·choo mee·k·hoo·*nah*·pahkh
ee·mah·*lyah*·pahs?

¿Kanchu mikhunapaq
imallapas?

What time do you want us to get up?
ee·mah oo·*rahs*·mee
hah·tah·ree·*koo*·mahn?

¿Ima urasmi
hatariykuman?

Can I help you with something?
pahkh·tah ee·mah·lyah·*tah*·pees
yah·nah·pai·*kee*·mahn?

¿Paqta imallatapis
yanapaykiman?

Can I leave my backpack here
until tonight/tomorrow?
sah·ke·*mahn*·choo
too·tah·*kah*·mah/
pah·kah·reen·*kah*·mah
k'e·*pee*·tah kai·pee?

¿Saqiymanchu
tutakama/
paqarinkama
q'ipiyta kaypi?

May I leave my luggage
here with you?
pahkh·tah mah·lee·*tai*·tah
sah·ke·yoo·kui·*kee*·mahn?

¿Paqta malitayta
saqiyukuykiman?

Could you lend me (a) ...?	*pahkh*·tah ....tah mah·nyah·wahn· *kee*·mahn?	¿Paqta ...-ta mañawan- nkiman?
blanket	*kah*·tah/free·*sah*·rah	qata/phrisara
bucket	*bahl*·dee	baldi
wash basin	poo·*roo*·nyah	puruña

COMPLAINTS

PIÑARIKUY

It's very ...	ahn·chah ...n	Ancha ...-n
cold	chee·ree	chiri
dark	too·tah	tuta
noisy	rokh·yah	ruqya

This ... is not clean.	mah·nahn kai ...kah pee·chas·kah·choo	Manan kay ...-qa pichasqachu
bed	poo·nyoo·nah	puñuna
blanket	kah·tah/free·sah·rah/ choo·see	qatal/frisaral chusi
house	wah·see	wasi
pillow	sow·nah	sawna
room	kwahr·too	kwartu
towel	ch'ah·kee·chee·koo·nah/ too·wah·lyah	ch'akichikuna/ tuwalla

ACCOMMODATION

HOMESTAYS

QURPACHAKUYKUNA

Homestays are common in smaller communities. In some cases, you may be able to arrange one through a travel agent in the city, but if you're the adventurous sort, you can always trust your luck and try to find one yourself.

Where can I find a place to stay tonight?

mai·pee·tahk poo·nyoo·pah·koo·rui·mahn?

¿Maypitaq puñupakurquyman?

Could I/we please spend the night in your house?

ah·lyee·choo poo·nyoo·pah·yoo· kui·kee·mahn·choo?;
ah·lyee·choo poo·nyoo·pah·yoo· kui·kee·koo·mahn·choo?

¿Allichu puñupayukuykimanchu?;
¿Allichu puñupayukuykikumanchu?

We have our own mattresses/ sleeping bags.

poo·nyui·nai·koo kahn·mee

Puñunayku kanmi.

ACCOMMODATION

How much do you charge for ...?	*hai·k'ahn kwees·tahn ...?*	¿Hayk'an kwistan ...?
each night	*sah·*pah *too·*tah	sapa tuta
each day	*sah·*pah *p'oon·*chai	sapa p'unchay
both of us	ees·kai·nee· *koo·*pahkh	iskayni-ykupaq

Thank you, I'd like to stay in your house.

sool·*pai·*kee, wah·see·*kee·*pee
kor·pah·*chai·*tahn
moo·*nai·*mahn

Sulpayki, wasiykipi qurpachaytan munayman.

THEY MAY SAY ...

ah·*lyeen·*mee, pah·sai·*kah·*mui
tai·*tai*/mah·*mai*
  That's OK. Come in sir/madam.

pahm·pah·chah·*yoo·*wai *mah·*nahn
poo·nyoo·*nai·*koo *kahn·*choo
  I'm sorry, but we don't have the room.

pahm·pah·chah·*yoo·*wai *mah·*nah
roo·nah·koo·*nah·*tah
qor·pah·chah·chee·*koo·*choo
  I'm sorry, but we don't take guests.

mai·ken·nee·kee·*koo·*nahn
qor·*pah·*chah·koon·*kee·*chees kai·*pee?
  How many of you would like to stay?

*hai·*k'ah *too·*tahn poo·nyoo·pah·koon·*kee·*chees?
  How many nights?

ACCOMMODATION

DEPARTURE

LLUQSIY

I'm/We're leaving now.
koo·*nahn*·kah
ree·poo·koo·*sahkh*·nyah/
ree·poo·koo·sahkh·*koo*·nyah

*Kunanqa
ripukusaqña/
ripukusaqkuña.*

Thank you for all your help.
sool·*pai* yah·nah·pah·wahs·
kai·kee·*mahn*·tah

*Sulpáy yanapawa-
sqaykimanta.*

Thank you for letting me stay
in your house.
sool·*pai* wah·see·*kee*·pee
kor·pah·chah·chee·wahs·
kai·kee·*mahn*·tah/
poo·nyoo·chee·wahs·
kai·kee·*mahn*·tah

*Sulpáy wasiykipi
qurpachachiwas
qaykimanta/
puñuchiwa-
sqaykimanta.*

I hope I can return someday.
ee·*chah*·pahs hai·*k'ahkh*·pahs
koo·tee·*mui*·mahn

*Ichapas hayk'aqpas
kutimuyman.*

It was great staying at your place.
seen·*chee*·tah koo·see·*koo*·nee
wah·see·*kee*·pee
kor·pah·chah·chee·wahs·
kai·kee·*mahn*·tah

*Sinchita kusikuni
wasiykipi
qurpachachiwas-
qaykimanta.*

How much do I owe you?
hai·*k'ah*·tahkh mah·noo·*kui*·kee?

¿Hayk'ataq manukuyki?

Here's payment for my stay.
kai kol·*ke*·tah koi·koo·*sai*·kee
wah·see·*kee*·pee
kor·pah·chah·chee·wahs·
kai·kee·*mahn*·tah

*Kay qulqita quykusayki
wasiykipi
qurpachachiwas-
qaykimanta.*

LLAQTAPI PURIY
AROUND TOWN

In some villages, Quechua will come in handy at archaeological tourist sites and in shops with Quechua names. Many of the typical nightlife activities and other forms of cosmopolitan entertainment in the larger Andean cities will be organised in Spanish or even in English. Signs will be in Spanish rather than Quechua.

LOOKING FOR ...   ... MASKHAY

Where's a/the ...?	mah·*pee*·tahkh ... kahn?	¿*Mapitaq* ... *kan?*
bank	*kol·keh wah*·see	*qulqi wasi*
hotel	*kor·pah wah*·see	*qurpa wasi*
main square	*plah*·sah	*plasa*
market	*k-hah*·too	*qhatu*
police station	wahr·*dee*·yah	*wardiya*
post office	koo·*ree*·yoo	*kuriyu*
public toilet	hees·*p'ah*·koo·nah/ *bah*·nyoo	*hisp'akuna/ bañu*
telephone centre	tee·lee·foo·*noo*·yokh *wah*·see	*tiliphunuyuq wasi*
local authorities' office (similar to a town hall)	kah·mah·chekh· koo·nahkh *wah*·seen	*kamachiq- kunaq wasin*

85

TELECOMMUNICATIONS

IMAYMANA WILLACHIKUYKUNA

Is there a/an ...	*kahn·*choo ...	*¿Kanchu ...*
in this village?	kai lyahkh·*tah·*pee?	*kay llaqtapi?*
computer	koom·poo·tah·*roo·*rah	*kumputarura*
Internet service	een·*teer·*neet	*Intirnit*
telephone	tee·lee·*foo·*noo	*tiliphunu*

It's urgent!	
oos·k·hai·*pahkh·*mee!;	*¡Usqhaypaqmi!;*
pree·see·sahkh·*pahkh·*mee!	*¡Prisisaqpaqmi!*

AROUND TOWN

Making a Call

Tiliphunuwan Rimay

Hello.	
nah·pai·koo·*lyai·*kee.	*Napaykullayki.*
This is ... speaking.	
...·n/·mee *kah·*nee	*...-n/-mi kani.*
I'd like to speak to ...	
...·*wahn·*mee ree·*mai·*tah moo·*nah·*nee	*...-wanmi rimayta munani.*
Who's calling?	
pee·*tahkh* *kahn·*kee?	*¿Pitaq kanki?*
Please tell ... I called.	
ah·*lyee·*choo ...·mahn wee·lyah·poo·*wahn·*kee tee·lee·foo·*noo·*pee wahkh·yah·moos·*kai·*tah	*Allichu ...-man willapuwanki tiliphunupi waqyamusqayta.*

SIGHTSEEING   TURISTAKUNA PURISQAN

Where's the tourist office?
mai·*pee*·tahkh
too·rees·tah·koo·*nah*·pahkh
oo·fee·*see*·nah *kah*·shahn?

*¿Maypitaq
turistakunapaq
ufisina kashan?*

What are the opening hours?
ee·mah oo·*rahs*·mee
kee·chah·*koon*·pees
wees·k'ah·*koon*·pees?

*¿Ima urasmi
kichakunpis
wisq'akunpis?*

How much is the entry fee?
hai·k'ahn *kwees*·tahn
yai·koo·*nah*·pahkh?

*¿Hayk'an kwistan
yaykunapaq?*

I'd like to see (Machu Picchu).
(*mah*·choo *peek*·choo)·tah
k·hah·*wai*·tah/rekh·*see*·tah
moo·*nai*·mahn

*(Machu Pikchu)-ta
qhawayta/riqsiyta
munayman.*

Can we take photographs here?
foo·too·koo·*nah*·tah
kor·koi·koo·*mahn*·choo
kai·pee?

*¿Phutukunata
qurquykumanchu
kaypi?*

Could we take photographs of you?
ah·*lyee*·choo foo·*too*·tah
kor·kor·koi·kee·*mahn*·choo?

*¿Allichu phututa
qurqurquykimanchu?*

Could you take a photograph of me?
ah·*lyee*·choo foo·*too*·tah
kor·kor·ko·wahn·
kee·*mahn*·choo?

*¿Allichu phututa
qurqurquwan-
kimanchu?*

I'll send you the photographs.
foo·too·koo·*nah*·tah
ah·pah·chee·moo·*sai*·kee

*Phutukunata
apachimusayki.*

It's ...	...n/·mee	...-n/-mi.
beautiful	*soo*·mahkh	*sumaq*
impressive	*koo*·sah *koo*·sah	*kusa kusa*
interesting	*seen*·chee ah·*lyeen*	*sinchi allin*
strange	hokh *rek*·ch'ahkh	*huq rikch'aq*

AROUND TOWN

AROUND TOWN

The Sights   ## Sumaq K'itikuna

What's that (building)?
  ee·*mah*·tahkh chai   ¿Imataq chay
  (*hah*·toon wah·*se*·kah)?   (hatun wasiqa)?
How old is that (building)?
  hai·k'ah wah·tah·*yokh*·mee ¿Hayk'a watayuqmi
  chai (*hah*·toon wah·*se*·kah)? chay hatun wasiqa?

aqueduct	*yahr*·k·hah	yarqha
archaeological	t-hoo·*nees*·kahkh *nyow*·pah	thunisqa ñawpa
site	wah·see·*koo*·nah	wasikuna
burial site	*chooly*·pah	chullpa
cathedral	*hah*·toon een·*lee*·sah	hatun inlisa
church	een·*lee*·sah	inlisa
cave	*mah*·ch'ai	mach'ay
cemetery	*ah*·yah pahm·*pah*·nah	aya pampana
central plaza	*hah*·toon *plah*·sah	hatun plasa
ceremonial	*een*·kahkh	Inkaq
baths	ahr·mah·*koo*·nahn	armakunan
crowded	*ahs*·k·hah	askha
	roo·nah·*koo*·nah	runakuna
dance	*too*·sui	tusuy
doorway	hai·*koo*·nah *poon*·koo	haykuna punku
festival	*rai*·mee	raymi
fortress	poo·*kah*·rah	pukara
gate	*hah*·toon *poon*·koo	hatun punku
Inca trail	*een*·kah poo·*rees*·kahn	Inka purisqan
	nyahn	ñan
monastery	*ahk*·lyah wah·see;	aklla wasi;
	moo·nahs·tee·*ree*·yoo	munastiriyu
museum	moo·*see*·yoo	musiyu
niche	*oos*·noo/*t'o*·ko	usnu/t'uqu
offering	hai·wah·*ree*·kui	haywarikuy
park	*pook*·lyah·nah *pahm*·pah;	puqllana pampa;
	pahr·kee	parki

principal temple	*hah*·toon *mahn*·kos *wah*·see	hatun manqus wasi
royal palace	*kees*·wahr/*hah*·toon *kahn*·chah	kiswar/hatun kancha
royal tomb	*chooly*·pah	chullpa
ruins	*rah*·kai *rah*·kai; t-hoo·*nees*·kah wah·see·*koo*·nah	raqay raqay; thunisqa wasikuna
settlement	*lyahkh*·tah/*ai*·lyoo	llaqta/ayllu
statue	*reek*·ch'ai/ ees·tah·*too*·wah	rikch'ay/ istatuwa
temple	*mahn*·kos *wah*·see	manqus wasi
temple of the Sun	ko·ree·*kahn*·chah	Qurikancha
textile/weaving	*ah*·wah	awa
volcano	*nee*·nah p-*hokh*·chekh *or*·ko	nina phuqchiq urqu
warrior	*ow*·kah *poo*·rekh	awqa puriq
window	k-hah·wah·*ree*·nah/*t'o*·ko	qhawarina/t'uqu

Tours

How much is a guide?
hai·*k'ah*·tahkh *koob*·rahn
poo·sai·*kah*·chahkh *roo*·nah?

Could we hire an English-speaking/
Spanish-speaking guide?
meen·k'ah·kui·koo·*mahn*·choo
een·lees/kahs·tee·*lyah*·noo
ree·mahkh poo·sai·kah·*chahkh*·tah?

I'm with them.
pai·koo·nah·*wahn*·mee
kah·*shah*·nee

I've lost my group.
too·rees·tah·mah·see·koo·*nah*·tahn
cheen·kah·chee·koor·*ko*·nee

Have you seen a group of foreigners?
k·hah·wahr·kahn·*kee*·choo
hah·wah roo·nah·koo·*nah*·tah?

Turistakuna Purinan

*¿Hayk'ataq kubran
pusaykachaq runa?*

*¿Mink'akuykumanchu
inlis/kastillanu
rimaq pusaykachaqta?*

*Paykunawanmi
kashani.*

*Turistamasikunatan
chinkachikurquni.*

*¿Qhawarqankichu
hawa runakunata?*

YOU SAY POTATO ...

Historically, there have been more than 80 distinct ways of writing the name of the Quechua language. This was due mostly to variations in regional pronunciations, and also to a misanalysis of the relationship between different sounds. Some examples: *cjeswa, kechwa, khetsua, kichwa, kkechuwa, keshua, keswa, qheswa, q'eswa, qhexwa, quichua* and *qqichua*. In modern times, with the increasing standardisation of the Quechua alphabet, some researchers have proposed the following spellings: *kichwa, qhiswa* and *qichwa.*

GOING OUT

'Going out' in smaller communities is generally limited to visiting neighbours or attending local festivities.

MAYTAPAS RIY

This place is great.
kai lyahkh·*tah*·kah/fees·*tah*·kah
seen·chee soo·*mahkh*·mee

Kay llaqtaqa/phistaqa sinchi sumaqmi.

I'm having a good time here.
k'o·choo·ree·koo·*shah*·neen
kai·pee

Q'uchurikushanin kaypi.

Shall we go somewhere else?
pahkh·tah mai·*tah*·pahs
reen·*chees*·mahn?

¿Paqta maytapas rinchisman?

I'm sorry, I'm a terrible dancer.
dees·peen·sah·*yoo*·wai, *mah*·nahn
koo·*sah*·tah too·soo·*nee*·choo

Dispinsayuwa, manan kusata tusunichu.

Where to Go

What's there to do in the evenings?
ee·mah·*tah*·tahkh roo·nah·*koo*·nah
too·*tah*·pee roo·*wahn*·koo
k'o·choo·ree·koo·nahn·*koo*·pahkh?

Maytan Rinkiman

¿Imatataq runakuna tutapi ruwanku q'uchurikunankupaq?

What shall we do tonight?
ee·mah·*tah*·tahkh
roo·wahn·*chees*·mahn
koo·nahn too·*tah*?

¿Imatataq ruwanchisman kunan tuta?

Are there musicians?
kahn·choo moo·see·koo·*koo*·nah?

¿Kanchu musikukuna?

I feel like going to a/the ...	...·man *ree*·tah moo·*nai*·mahn	...-man riyta munayman.
chicha bar	*ah*·k·hah *wah*·see	aqha wasi
local fiesta	kai lyahkh·*tah*·pee *fees*·tah	kay llaqtapi phista
restaurant	mee·*k·hoo*·nah *wah*·see	mikhuna wasi

I'd like to ...	...·tah moo·*nai*·mahn	...-ta munayman.
dance	*too*·sui	tusuy
drink coffee/	*kah*·fee/	kaphiy/
tea	*tee*·tah *ook*·yai	tiyta ukyay
walk	*poo*·ree	puriy

Invitations   Inwitasiyunkuna

What are you doing this evening?
ee·mah·*tah*·tahkh *koo*·nahn *too*·tah roo·*wahn*·kee?

¿Imatataq kunan tuta ruwanki?

Would you like to go out somewhere today/tomorrow?
mai·*tah*·pahs *ree*·tah moo·nahn·kee·*mahn*·choo *koo*·nahn/pah·*kah*·reen?

¿Maytapas riyta munankimanchu kunan/paqarin?

Would you like to go for a drink?
ee·mah·lyah·*tah*·pees ook·yah·*nah*·pahkh mai·*tah*·pees *ree*·tah moo·nahn·kee·*mahn*·choo?

¿Imallatapis ukyanapaq maytapis riyta munankimanchu?

Would you like to go for a meal?
ee·mah·lyah·*tah*·pees mee·k·hoo·*nah*·pahkh mai·*tah*·pees *ree*·tah moo·nahn·kee·*mahn*·choo?

¿Imallatapis mikhunapaq maytapis riyta munankimanchu?

Do you know a good restaurant?
rekh·seen·*kee*·choo hokh *soo*·makh mee·*k·hoo*·nah wah·*see*·tah?

¿Riqsinkichu huq sumaq mikhuna wasita?

My shout/treat. (I'll buy)
    no·kahn een·wee·tah·*sai*·kee

    Nuqan inwitasayki.

Do you want to go to the ...?
    ...·tah *ree*·tah
    moo·nahn·*kee*·choo?

    ¿...-ta riyta
    munankichu?

Come on!/Let's go!
    hah·koo!/hah·*koo*·chee!

    ¡Haku!/¡Hakuchi!

Responding to Invitations

Inwitasiyunkunata Kutichiy

Sure!
    ah·*lyeen*·mee!

    ¡Allinmi!

Yes, I'd love to.
    ah·*ree*, moo·nai·*mahn*·mee

    Arí, munaymanmi.

Yes. Where shall we go?
    ah·*ree*. mai·*tah*·tahkh
    reen·*chees*·mahn?

    Arí. ¿Maytataq
    rinchisman?

No. I'm afraid I can't.
    mah·nahn *ree*·tah
    ah·tee·*nee*·choo

    Manan riyta
    atinichu.

I don't have time.
    mah·nahn *teem*·pui *kahn*·choo

    Manan timpuy kanchu.

What about tomorrow?
    ee·mah·*tah*·tahkh roo·*wahn*·kee
    pah·*kah*·reen?

    ¿Imatataq ruwanki
    paqarin?

Arranging to Meet

Tinkunapaq Rimanakuy

What time shall we meet?
    ee·mah oo·*rahs*·mee
    teen·koo·*soon*·chees?

    ¿Ima urasmi
    tinkusunchis?

Where shall we meet?
    mai·peen teen·koo·*soon*·chees?

    ¿Maypin tinkusunchis?

Let's meet (at eight o'clock) at the ...
    (lahs *oo*·choo oo·*rahs*·tah)
    teen·*koo*·soon ....pee

    (Las uchu urasta)
    Tinkusun ...-pi.

OK. I'll see you then.
   *koo·*sah
   too·pahn·ahn·chees·*kah·*mah

Kusa.
Tupananchiskama.

Agreed!/OK!
   ah·*lyeen·*mee!/*koo·*sah!

¡Allinmi!/¡Kusa!

I'll come over at (six/eight) o'clock.
   (lahs *sah·*yees/lahs *oo·*choo)
   oo·*rahs·*tah hah·*moo·*sahkh

(Las sayis/Las uchu)
Urasta hamusaq.

I'll try to make it.
   ah·*tees·*pah *mah·*nah
   ah·tees·*pah·*pees
   hah·moo·*sahkh·*mee

Atispa mana
atispapis
hamusaqmi.

I'll be along later.
   *ahs·*wahn k·he·pah·tah·*rahkh·*mee
   hah·*moo·*sahkh

Aswan qhipataraqmi
hamusaq.

Where will you be?
   *mai·*peen *kahn·*kee?

¿Maypin kanki?

See you later/tomorrow.
   too·pah·nahn·chees·*kah·*mah/
   pah·kah·reen·*kah·*mah

Tupananchiskama/
Paqarinkama.

Sorry I'm late.
   pahm·pah·chah·*yoo·*wai
   k·he·pah·ree·koos·khai·*mahn·*tah

Pampachayuway
qhiparikusqaymanta.

FAMILY

The family is the highest priority for every individual in Andean society. Extended families are the norm, with parents, children, grandparents and sometimes other relatives living together. Kinship often extends beyond the biological family through marriage and a system where godparents are expected to act as a second set of parents to a child. The more children you have, the more godparents, and thus the larger the extended family and community, known as an *ayllu*, ai·lyoo.

Romantic relationships, marital status and children are common topics of conversation for young people.

QUESTIONS & ANSWERS
TAPUYKUNAPIS KUTICHIYKUNAPIS

Are you married? (asked to a woman)

ko·sah·*yokh*·choo/
kah·sah·*roo*·choo kahn·kee?

¿Qusayuqchu/
Kasaruchu kanki?

Are you married? (asked to a man)

wahr·mee·*yokh*·choo/
kah·sah·*roo*·choo kahn·kee?

¿Warmiyuqchu/
Kasaruchu kanki?

I'm (a) ...	*no*·kah ...·n/·mee *kah*·nee	Nuqa ...·n/·mi kani.
divorced	t'ah·qah·nah·*koos*·kah/ t'ah·*kahs*·kah	*t'aqanakusqa/ t'aqasqa*
married (f)	ko·*sah*·yokh	*qusayuq*
married (m)	wahr·*mee*·yokh	*warmiyuq*
separated	t'ah·*kahs*·kah	*t'aqasqa*
single (f)	sool·*tee*·rah; mah·nah ko·*sah*·yokh	*sultira; mana qusayuq*
single (m)	sool·*tee*·roo; mah·nah wahr·*mee*·yokh	*sultiru; mana warmiyuq*
widow	*wahr*·mee sah·pah	*warmi sapa*
widower	sah·pahn k·*hah*·ree	*sapan qhari*

I have a partner.
   yah·nah·*yokh*·mee *kah*·nee   *Yanayuqmi kani.*

We live together
but we're not married.
   no·*kai*·koo koos·*kai*·koon   *Nuqayku kuskaykun*
   tee·*yai*·koo,   *tiyayku,*
   ee·*chah*·kah *mah*·nahn   *ichaqa manan*
   kah·sah·rah·koos·*kah*·choo *kai*·koo *kasarakusqachu kayku.*

The word 'child' isn't used by men, who must always specify the sex of their children. Women, however, can be asked or might say these phrases:

How many ... do you have?	*hai*·k'ahn ...?	¿*Hayk'an ...?*
children	wah·wai·kee·*koo*·nah	*wawaykikuna*
sons	k·*hah*·ree	*qhari*
	wah·wai·kee·*koo*·nah	*wawaykikuna*
daughters	*wahr*·mee	*warmi*
	wah·wai·kee·*koo*·nah	*wawaykikuna*

I don't have any children.
   mah·nahn wah·wai·*koo*·nai   *Manan wawaykunay.*

I have ... daughter(s)/son(s).
   ...·n/·mee *wahr*·mee/k·*hah*·ree   *...-n/-mi warmi/qhari*
   wah·wai(*koo*·nah)   *waway(kuna).*

How many brothers/sisters
do you have?
   hai·k'ahn too·rai·kee·*koo*·nah/ ¿*Hayk'an turaykikuna/*
   nyah·nyai·kee·*koo*·nah?   *ñañaykikuna?*

Men can be asked or might say these phrases:

How many ... do you have?	*hai*·k'ahn ...?	¿*Hayk'an ...?*
sons	choo·ree·*koo*·nah	*churiykuna*
daughters	oo·soo·see·kee·*koo*·nah	*ususiykikuna*

I don't have any sons/daughters.
    mah·nahn choo·ree·*koo*·nah/   *Manan churiykuna/*
    oo·*soo*·see·*koo*·nah *kahn*·choo   *ususiykuna kanchu.*

I have ... daughter(s)/son(s).
    ...·n/·*mee* choo·ree*(koo*·nah)/   *...-n/-mi churiy(kuna)/*
    oo·*soo*·see*(koo*·nah)   *ususiy(kuna).*

How many brothers/sisters
do you have?
    hai·k'ahn wow·kay·kee·*koo*·nah/   *¿Hayk'an wawqiykikuna/*
    pah·nai·kee·*koo*·nah?   *panaykikuna?*

Both men and women can be asked or might say:

How old are they?
    hai·k'ah wah·tah·*yokh*·mee   *¿Hayk'a watayuqmi*
    pai·*koo*·nah *kahn*·koo?   *paykuna kanku?*

Do you live with your family?
    ai·lyui·kee·*wahn*·choo/   *¿Aylluykiwanchu/*
    fah·mee·lyai·kee·*wahn*·choo   *phamillaykiwanchu*
    tee·*yahn*·kee?   *tiyanki?*

I live with my family.
    ai·lyui·*wahn*·mee tee·*yah*·nee   *Aylluywanmi tiyani.*

Do you have a girlfriend/boyfriend?
    yah·nah·*yokh*·choo *kahn*·kee?   *¿Yanayuqchu kanki?*

THE PERFECT ENDING

Remember, when using the *-n/-mi* suffix, choose
the *-n* ending when the preceding root word ends
in a vowel, and the *-mi* ending when it ends in
a consonant. Note that using the *-mi* ending
will change which syllable is stressed. This is a
general rule in this book.

FAMILY

FAMILY MEMBERS   AYLLUKUNA

aunt	*tee*·yah	*tiya*
baby	*wah*·wah/	*wawa/*
	wah·*wah*·chah	*wawacha*
boy	er·kel*makh*·tah	*irqi/maqta*
boyfriend	*yah*·nah	*yana*
brother (of a woman)	*too*·rah/*too*·ree	*tura/turi*
brother (of a man)	wai·kel*wow*·ke	*wayqi/wawqi*
child (of a woman)	*wah*·wah	*wawa*
daughter (of a woman)	*wahr*·mee *wah*·wah	*warmi wawa*
daughter (of a man)	oo·*soo*·see;	*ususi;*
	wahr·mee *choo*·ree	*warmi churi*
family	*ai*·lyoo/	*ayllu/*
	fah·*mee*·lyah	*phamilla*
father	*tai*·tah/*pah*·pah/	*tayta/papa/*
	tah·tah	*tata*
father-in-law	*sui*·roo	*suyru*
girl	*p'ahs*·nyah/*see*·pahs/	*p'asña/sipas/*
	see·*pahs*·chah	*sipascha*
girlfriend	*yah*·nah	*yana*
grandchild	*hah*·wai	*haway*
grandfather	*hah*·toon *tai*·tah	*hatun tayta*
	ah·*poo*·chah;	*apucha;*
	mah·*choo*·lah;	*machula;*
	hah·*too*·koo;	*hatuku;*
	ah·*wee*·loo	*awilu*
grandmother	*hah*·toon *mah*·mah;	*hatun mama;*
	ah·*wee*·lah	*awila*
husband	*ko*·sah	*qusa*
mother	*mah*·mah	*mama*
mother-in-law	*sui*·rah	*suyra*
parents	tai·tah·*mah*·mah	*taytamama*
sister (of a woman)	*nyah*·nyah	*ñaña*
sister (of a man)	*pah*·nah/*pah*·nee	*pana/pani*
son (of a woman)	k·*hah*·ree *wah*·wah	*qhari wawa*

son (of a man)	*choo*·ree	*churi*
stepfather	*k-he*·pah *tai*·tah	*qhipa tayta*
stepmother	*k-he*·pah *mah*·mah	*qhipa mama*
uncle	*tee*·yoo	*tiyu*
wife	*wahr*·mee	*warmi*

TALKING WITH PARENTS

TAYTAMAMAKUNAWAN RIMAY

When's the baby due?
   hai·*k'ahkh*·mee
   wah·chah·*koon*·kee?

¿Hayk'aqmi
wachakunki?

What are you going to call
your baby?
   ee·*mah*·tahkh wah·*wai*·kekh
   soo·teen *kahñ*·kah?

¿Imataq wawaykiq
sutin kanqa?

Women can be asked or might say these phrases:

Is this your first child?
   p-hee·wee
   wah·wai·*kee*·choo pai?

¿Phiwi
wawaykichu pay?

How old are your children?
   hai·k'ah wah·tah·*yohkh*·mee
   wah·wai·kee·*koo*·nah?

¿Hayk'a watayuqmi
wawaykikuna?

Men can be asked or might say:

How old are your sons/daughters?
   hai·k'ah wah·tah·*yohkh*·mee
   choo·ree·kee·*koo*·nah/
   oo·soo·see·kee·*koo*·nah?

¿Hayk'a watayuqmi
churiykikuna/
ususiykikuna?

FAMILY

FAMILY FAVOURS

Mutual cooperation among families and members of the *aylu, ai·lyoo*, 'extended family', is a way of life. *Ayni, ai·nee*, 'reciprocal labour', assures that if you do someone a favour or lend them something today, they'll return the favour tomorrow. A similar concept is *mink'a, meen·k'ah*, which means 'cooperation' or 'collaboration'.

Incredible! You look so young!
  *mah·*nah ee·*nyee·*nah!   ¡Mana iñina!
  *see·*pahs/*wai·*nah   Sipas/Wayna
  *hee·*nah kah·*shahm·*kee   hina kashanki.

Does she/he attend school?
  *yah·*chai wah·*see·*tah reen·choo?   ¿Yachay wasita rinchu?

Who looks after the children?
  *pee·*tahkh   ¿Pitaq
  wahr·mah·chah·koo·*nah·*tah   warmachakunata
  k·*hah·*wahn?   qhawan?

Do you have grandchildren?
  hah·wai·kee·koo·nah *kahm·*choo? ¿Hawaykikuna kanchu?

What's your baby's name?
  ee·*mah·*tahkh wah·wah·*chai·*kekh ¡Imataq wawachaykiq
  *soo·*teen?   sutin?

Is it a boy or a girl?
  er·*ke·*choo ee·*chah*   ¿Irqichu icha
  p'ahs·*nyah·*choo?   p'asñachu?

Does she/he let you sleep at night?
  poo·*nyoon·*choo too·*tah·*pee? ¿Puñunchu tutapi?

What a beautiful child!
  ee·mah soo·makh *wah·*wah!   ¡Ima sumaq wawa!

She/He looks like you.
  *pai·*kah kahn·*mahn·*mee   Payqa qanmanmi
  reekh·*ch'ah·*koon   rikch'akun.

FAMILY

TALKING WITH CHILDREN

WARMAKUNAWAN RIMAY

What's your name?
ee·mahn soo·*tee*·kee?

¿Iman sutiyki?

How old are you?
hai·k'ah wah·tah·chah·*yokh*·mee
kahn·kee?

*¿Hayk'a watachayuqmi
kanki?*

When's your birthday?
hai·*k'ahkh*·mee
wah·t'a hoon·t'ai·*nee*·kee?

*¿Hayk'aqmi
wat'a hunt'ayniki?*

Do you have brothers and sisters?
(said to a girl)
too·rah·nyah·nyah·*yokh*·choo
kahn·kee?

*¿Tura-ñañayuqchu
kanki?*

Do you have brothers and sisters?
(said to a boy)
wow·ke·pah·nah·*yokh*·choo
kahn·kee?

*¿Wawqi-panayuqchu
kanki?*

Do you go to school?
yah·chai wah·*see*·tah/
ees·kui·*lah*·tah reen·*kee*·choo?

*¿Yachay wasita/
iskuylata rinkichu?*

Do you like school?
moo·nahn·*kee*·choo *yah*·chai
wah·*see*·tah/ees·kui·*lah*·tah?

*¿Munankichu yachay
wasita/iskuylata?*

Is your teacher nice?
ah·lyeen roo·*nah*·choo
yah·chah·chekh·*nee*·kee?

*¿Allin runachu
yachachiqniyki?*

Do you play soccer?
pee·*loo*·tah hai·*t'ai*·tah
pookh·lyahn·*kee*·choo?

*¿Piluta hayt'ayta
pukllankichu?*

What kind of games do you play?
ee·mah
pookh·lyai·koo·*nah*·tahn
pookh·*lyahn*·kee?

*¿Ima
pukllaykunatan
pukllanki?*

Do you study English?
een·lees see·*mee*·tah
yah·chahn·*kee*·choo?

*¿Inlis simita
yachankichu?*

Do you want to play?
   pookh·*lyai*·tah
   moo·nahn·*kee*·choo?

¿Pukllayta
munankichu?

What shall we play?
   ee·mah·*tah*·tahkh
   pookh·lyahn·*chees*·mahn?

¿Imatataq
pukllanchisman?

Do you have a pet at home?
   chee·*tai*·kee *kahn*·choo
   wah·see·*kee*·pee?

¿Chitayki kanchu
wasiykipi?

MUNASQANCHISKUNAPAS RUWANANCHISKUNAPAS
INTERESTS & ACTIVITIES

Some activities that Westerners think of as hobbies, such as gardening, walking and cooking, are still very much a way of life for Andean people.

COMMON INTERESTS		KAQLLA MUNASQANCHISKUNA
What do you do in your spare time?		
	ee·mah·*tah*·tahkh roo·*wahn*·kee teem·*pui*·kee kahkh·teen?	¿Imatataq ruwanki timpuyki kaqtin?
Do you like ...?	...tah moo·nahn·*kee*·choo?	¿...-ta munankichu?
I like ...	...tah moo·*nah*·neen.	...-ta munanin.
I don't like ...	*mah*·nahn ...tah moo·nah·*nee*·choo	Manan ...-ta munanichu.
cooking	*wai*·k'ui	wayk'uy
dancing	*too*·sui	tusuy
fishing	*chahly*·wai; chahly·*wah*·kui; *chahly*·wah hah·p'ee	challway; challwakuy; challwa hap'iy
food	mee·*k·hoo*·nah	mikhuna
getting together with friends	k·hoo·yah·nah·kokh·mah·see·koo·*nah*·wahn hoo·nyoo·*nah*·kui	khuyanakuq-masikunawan huñunakuy
hiking	*poo*·ree	puriy
hunting	*hah*·p'ee/*chah*·kui	hap'iy/chakuy
music	moo·*see*·kah	musika
reading	*lee*·yee/ nyah·*ween*·chai	liyiy/ ñawinchay
singing	*tah*·kee	takiy
talking	*ree*·mai	rimay

INTERESTS & ACTIVITIES

I make ...	...tahn roo·*wah*·nee	...-tan ruwani
clothes	p'ah·chah·*koo*·nah	*p'achakuna*
embroidery	*wel*·k'oy	*wilq'uy*
handicrafts	ahr·tee·sah·*nee*·yah	*artisaniya*
jewellery	ee·lyah/oo·*mee*·nyah	*illa/umiña*
pottery	*rakh*·ch'ee/*k'akh*·rah	*raqch'i/k'akra*
textiles	ah·wai·*koo*·nah	*awaykuna*

carve (only stone)	*koo*·chui/*ch'e*·koi	*kuchuy/ch'iquy*
draw	se·*ken*·chai	*siq'inchay*
embroider	*wel*·k'oy	*wilq'uy*
paint	*lyoo*·see/*peen*·tai	*llusiy/pintay*
sew	*see*·rai	*siray*
spin (thread or yarn)	*pooch*·kai/*poos*·kai	*puchkay/puskay*
weave	*ah*·wai	*away*

SPORT

PUKLLAYKUNA

What sport do you play?
ee·mah pookh·*lyai*·koo·*nah*·tahn pookh·*lyan*·kee?

¿Ima pukllaykunatan pukllanki?

I play soccer/volleyball.
[pee·*loo*·tah hai·*t'ai*·tah; boo·*lee*·tah] pookh·*lyah*·nee

[piluta hayt'ay-ta; bulita] pukllani.

I can swim.
wai·*t'ai*·tah yah·*chah*·nee

Wayt'ayta yachani.

I like to run.
pah·*wai*·tahn moo·*nah*·nee

Pawaytan munani.

I like fishing.
chahly·wah hah·*p'ee*·tahn moo·*nah*·nee

Challwa hap'itan munani.

I know how to bullfight.
too·roo pookh·*lyai*·tah yah·*chah*·nee

Turu pukllayta yachani.

Do you like sports?
    pook·lyai·koo·*nah*·tah   *¿Pukllaykunata*
    moo·nahn·*kee*·choo?   *munankichu?*
Yes, very much.
    ah·*ree*, ahn·*chah*·tahn   *Arí, anchatan*
    moo·*nah*·nee   *munani.*
No, not at all.
    mah·nahn moo·nah·*nee*·choo   *Manan munanichu.*
I like watching sport.
    k-hah·wai·*lyah*·tah moo·*nah*·nee   *Qhawayllata munani.*

Talking about Soccer

Piluta Hayt'aymanta Rimay

Do you follow soccer?
    pee·*loo*·tah hai·*t'ai*·tah   *¿Piluta hayt'ayta*
    pah·sahkh koo·*tee*·lyah   *pasaq kutilla*
    k-hah·wahn·*kee*·choo?   *qhawankichu?*
Which team do you support?
    mai·ken·*neen*·tahkh   *¿Mayqinnintaq*
    ee·kee·*pui*·kee?   *ikipuyki?*
Who's winning?
    mai·ken·*neen*·tahkh   *¿Mayqinnintaq*
    lyah·*lyee*·shahn?   *llallishan?*
Do you play in a team?
    ee·kee·*poo*·pee   *¿Ikipupi*
    pookh·lyahn·*kee*·choo?   *pukllankichu?*
Do you want to play soccer?
    pee·*loo*·tah hai·*t'ai*·tah   *¿Piluta hayt'ayta*
    moo·nahn·*kee*·choo?   *munankichu?*

THEY MAY YELL ...

gool!		Goal!
pee·nahl!		Penalty!
ow·sai!		Offside!
tee·roo *lyoo*·ree!		Free kick!

MUSIC   *MUSIKA*

Traditional Andean music takes a variety of forms. The best known include the *waynu*, *wai·*noo, which can be fast or slow, happy or sad; the *harawi*, hah·*rah·*wee, typically a sweet but sad song; the *waylas*, *wai·*lahs, a fast melody; and the *sikuri*, see·*koo·*ree, which starts out slowly but gradually increases in tempo. It's often used to express Andean spiritual tradition and is popular in worship ceremonies. Each style of music is performed using distinctive instruments, and has its own dance variations.

The *cumbia*, *koom·*bya, is popular throughout the Andes, as is the *chicha*, *chee·*chah, genre: a mixture of coastal *cumbia* and the *waynu* (not to be confused with the popular drink *chicha*).

RATTLE AND HUM

Since pre-Columbian times, the instruments of the Andes have included various types of panpipes, flutes, drums, a guitar-like instrument made from an armadillo shell and leg rattles made of pig or goat hooves. In modern times, guitars, violins and harps have been added to the traditional repertoire of instruments, encouraging innovation in the styles and rhythms of Andean music.

Generally, Quechua speakers are very pleased to talk about music and instruments, as they have profound meaning in their lives.

antara/rundadur   ahn·*tah·*rah/roon·*dah·*door
  panpipe of bamboo, with a single row of pipes.
  It's called a *rundadur* in Ecuador only.
chaqchas/chullus   chahkh·chahs/choo·lyoos
  Bolivian leg rattle, made of ribbon with goat or pig
  hooves woven onto it

INTERESTS &
ACTIVITIES

RATTLE AND HUM (cont.)

charangu/kirkinchu   chah·*rahn*·goo/
                         keer·*keen*·choo
  small Andean ten-string guitar, made of armadillo
  shell or carved wood

harpa   *hahr*·pah
  harp

kañari/   kah·*nyah*·ree/
waqraphuku   wahkh·rah·*p-hoo*·koo
  Andean horn, made from a cow's horn

pinkuyllu   peen·*kui*·lyoo
  Andean long flute, made from hardwood

pututu   poo·*too*·too
  conch shell horn

qina   *ke*·nah
  Andean flute, made from bone or hardwood

siku   *see*·koo
  panpipe of cane or bamboo, with two rows of pipes

tinya   *teen*·yah
  tambourine or small drum, made from tree bark and
  goat skin

ukarina   oo·kah·*ree*·nah
  Andean globular flute

wankar   *wahn*·kahr
  mid-sized Andean drum of sheep skin

wankara   wahn·*kah*·rah
  large, round Andean drum, made of wood, shell and
  goat skin

waylachu   wai·*lah*·choo
  devil *charango*; has metal strings that produce a
  sharp sound

wiyulin   wee·*yoo*·leen
  violin or fiddle

INTERESTS & ACTIVITIES

Do you like ...?	...tah moo·nahn·*kee*·choo?	¿...-ta munankichu?
listening to music	moo·see·*kah*·tah	musikata
dancing	oo·*yah*·ree	uyariy
	too·sui	tusuy

Do you know how to play ...?
...tah wah·kah·cheen·*kee*·choo?   ¿...-ta waqachinkichu?

I play ...
...tah wah·kah·*chee*·nee   ...-ta waqachini.

Where can I hear traditional music around here?
mai·*pee*·tahkh see·koo·ree·koo·*nah*·tah oo·yah·reer·*koi*·mahn kai lyahkh·*tah*·pee?

¿Maypitaq sikurikunata uyarirquyman kay llaqtapi?

INTERESTS & ACTIVITIES

TALKING ABOUT TRAVELLING

PURIYMANTA RIMAY

I've been travelling for (two) months.
  (ees)·kai kee·*lyah*·nyahn
  poo·*ree*·lyah poo·ree·*koo*·nee

(Iskay) killañan purilla purikuni.

I'm going to ...
  ...·*sahkh*·mee

...-saqmi.

I've been to ...
  ...·pee poo·ree·moor·*kah*·nee

...-pi purimurqani.

Is it safe for women travellers on their own?
  ah·*leen*·choo sah·pah·*lyahn*·koo
  wahr·mee·*koo*·nah *chai*·pee
  poo·ree·moo·nahn·*koo*·pahkh?

¿Allinchu sapallanku warmikuna chaypi purimunankupaq?

I thought
it was ...
  boring
  great
  horrible
  OK
  too expensive

...·*ch*/·chah chai
nees·pah nee·nee
  mah·nah ah·*lyeen*
  ee·mah *soo*·mahkh
  mee·lyai
  koo·sah
  ahn·chah chah·nee·yokh

...-ch/-chay nispa nini.
  mana allin
  ima sumaq
  millay
  kusa
  ancha chaniyuq

STAYING IN TOUCH

ATUNAKUKUY

Tomorrow is my last day here.
  pah·kah·reen·kah·*mah*·lyahn
  kai·pee kah·sahkh

Paqarinkamallan kaypi kasaq.

Let's swap addresses.
  dee·reek·see·*yoon*·neen·*chees*·tah
  koi·koo·nah·koo·soon·*yah*

Diriksiyunninchista quykunakusunyá.

I'll send you copies of the photos.
  foo·too·*koo*·nahkh
  koo·pee·*yahn*·tah
  ah·pah·chee·moo·*sai*·keen

Phutukunaq kupiyanta apachimusaykin.

I'll write to you.
  kel·kah·moo·*sai*·keen

Qilqamusaykin.

INTERESTS &
ACTIVITIES

It's been great meeting you.

ahn·*chah*·tahn koo·see·*koo*·nee
rekh·see·koos·*pai*·kee

*Anchatan kusikuni
riqsikuspayki.*

Keep in touch!

kel·kah·nah·koo·soon·*yah!*/
wah·too·nah·koo·koo·soon·*yah!*

*¡Qilqanakusunyá!/
¡Watunakukusunyá!*

PUTTING THE RECORD STRAIGHT

The early colonial period (1532–1820s) produced two important literary works by *misti, mees-tee,* mixed-blood authors, still well known today.

The Royal Commentaries of the Incas and General History of Peru (1609), by Garcilaso de la Vega, compares the greatness of the Inca civilization with the great classical civilizations of Western history. The author, the son of an Inca princess and a Spanish conquistador, felt the need to validate his indigenous heritage through comparison with his Spanish roots. While the work is in Spanish, it's main thrust is to glorify the Inca empire, putting it on par with the Roman empire that gave rise to the Spanish empire.

The second work is *New Chronicle and Good Government* (1615), by Felipe Guaman Poma de Ayala. His 1300-page letter to the Spanish king is written in a complex combination of Spanish and Quechua, interspersed with other indigenous languages. He offers anecdotes from indigenous life before the conquest, to illustrate how poorly the King's representatives in the New World were faring in their administrative tasks.

Wilderness adventures and trekking are excellent ways to explore some of the more remote communities and archaeological sites. Companies based in highland cities specialise in arranging treks and mountain climbing expeditions. The local guides and porters often speak Quechua.

GETTING INFORMATION   TAPUKUY

Where can I find out about
hiking trails in the region?
   pee·*tah*·tahkh tah·*pui*·mahn
   kai lyahkh·*tah*·pee poo·*ree*·nah
   nyahn·koo·nah·*mahn*·tah?

*¿Pitataq tapuyman
kay llaqtapi purina
ñankunamanta?*

Who knows the hiking trails?
   pee·tahkh poo·*ree*·nah
   nyahn·koo·*nah*·tah *rekh*·seen?

*¿Pitaq purina
ñankunata riqsin?*

Do we need a guide?
   moo·nai·koo·*mahn*·choo
   nyahn rekh·see·*chekh*·tah?

*¿Munaykumanchu
ñan riqsichiqta?*

Are there guided treks here?
   kahn·choo nyahn
   rekh·see·chekh·*koo*·nah *kai*·pee?

*¿Kanchu ñan
riqsichiqkuna kaypi?*

Will you guide me?
   poo·sah·wahn·kee·*mahn*·choo?

¿Pusawankimanchu?

How long is the trail?
   mai·kah·*mah*·tahkh
   poo·reen·*chees*·mahn?

*¿Maykamataq
purinchisman?*

Is the track well-marked?
   ah·lyeen oo·nahn·chahs·*kah*·choo
   chai nyahn?

*¿Allin unanchasqachu
chay ñan?*

Which is the shortest route?
   mai·*ken*·tahkh *ahs*·wahn
   pee·see poo·*ree*·nah?

*¿Mayqintaq aswan
pisi purina?*

Which is the easiest route?
   mai·*ken*·tahkh *mah*·nah
   sah·sah poo·*ree*·nah?

*¿Mayqintaq mana
sasa purina?*

TREKKING

ALTITUDE SICKNESS

Altitude sickness, *suruchi*, soo·*roo*·chee, is always a real concern when travelling anywhere in the Andes. Symptoms include:

breathlessness	*mana samayniyuq*
	mah·nah sah·mai·*nee*·yokh
dizziness	*uma muyuy*
	oo·mah *moo*·yui
fatigue	*sayk'uy*
	sai·k'ui
headache	*uma nanay*
	oo·mah *nah*·nai
insomnia	*mana puñuy atipay*
	mah·nah poo·nyui ah·*tee*·pai
mental confusion	*yuyay pantay*
	yoo·yai *pahn*·tai
nausea	*millanayay*
	mee·lyah·*nah*·yai
a pounding heart	*sunqu phatatatay*
	son·ko p-hah·tah·*tah*·tai

If you're on the trail and start to notice symptoms, try to move to a lower altitude immediately. Glucose tablets may also help. Chewing coca leaves, *kuka matu*, koo·kah *mah*·too, is a local remedy that Andeans have used for centuries. If you can't bring yourself to do that, coca leaf tea, *kuka mati*, koo·kah *mah*·tee, might also do the trick. If you're in a city and you experience symptoms, rest and get acclimatised – drink plenty of water – before trying any strenuous activities such as trekking, even for short day trips. Seek medical assistance if the symptoms persist.

How many hours will it take?
    hai·k'ah oo·rahs·peen   ¿Hayk'a uraspin
    chai·mahn chah·yahn·chees?   chayman chayanchis?

Is the path open?
    kee·chahs·kah·choo   ¿Kichasqachu
    nyahn kah·shahn?   ñan kashan?

Is it safe to climb this mountain?
    wee·chah·nah·pahkh   ¿Wichanapaq
    ah·lyeen·choo kai or·ko?   allinchu kay urqu?

How high is the climb?
    mai·kah·mah·tahkh   ¿Maykamataq
    wee·chahn·chees·mahn?   wichanchisman?

Is there a hut up there?
    chookh·lyah kahn·choo   ¿Chuklla kanchu
    hah·nahkh·pee?   hanaqpi?

TREKKING

When does it get dark?
    ee·mah oo·rahs·mee   ¿Ima urasmi
    too·tah·yahn?   tutayan?

Where can I hire mountain gear?
    mai·pee·tahkh or·ko   ¿Maypitaq urqu
    wee·chah·nah·pahkh   wichanapaq
    ee·mah·tah·pahs   imatapas
    ahl·kee·lah·rui·mahn?   alkilarquyman?

Where can we buy supplies?
    mai·pee·tahkh ee·mai·mah·nah ¿Maypitaq imaymana
    kahkh·koo·nah·tah   kaqkunata
    rahn·tee·rui·koo·mahn?   rantirquykuman?

Do you have llamas?
    kahn·choo   ¿Kanchu
    lyah·mai·kee·koo·nah?   llamaykikuna?

How much do you charge for ...?	hai·*k'ah*·tahn koob·*rahn*·kee ...?	¿Hayk'atan kubranki ...?
a day	*sah*·pah p'oon·chai	sapa p'unchay
donkeys	ahs·nui·kee·koo·nah·*mahn*·tah	asnuykikuna-manta
llamas	lyah·mai·kee·koo·nah·*mahn*·tah	llamaykikuna-manta
mules	moo·lai·kee·koo·nah·*mahn*·tah	mulaykikuna-manta
a tent	kahr·pai·kee·*mahn*·tah	karpaykimanta

ON THE PATH   ÑANPI

Could you tell me the way to ...?
mai·*teen*·tahn ...·mahn *reen*·chees?
¿Maynintan ...-man rinchis?

Does this path go to ...?
...·mahn *reen*·choo kai nyahn?
¿...-man rinchu kay ñan?

Where have you come from?
mai·mahn·*tah*·tahkh hah·moo·*rahn*·kee?
¿Maymantataq hamurqanki?

How long did it take you?
hai·k'ah p'oon·chai·*pee*·tahkh chah·yah·rah·*moon*·kee?
¿Hayk'a p'unchaypitaq chayarqamunki?

Where's the nearest village?
mai·*pee*·tahkh kah·shahn lyoo·*mahn*·tah ahs·wahn *sees*·pah lyahkh·*tah*·kah?
¿Maypitaq kashan lliwmanta aswan sispa llaqtaqa?

Where can we spend the night?
mai·*pee*·tahkh poo·nyoo·pah·koo·yoo·*kui*·mahn?
¿Maypitaq puñupakuyukuyman?

Can I leave some things here for a while?
pahkh·tah rah·too·kah·*mah*·lyah k'e·pee·koo·*nah*·tah sah·ke·yoo·kui·*kee*·mahn *kai*·pee?
¿Paqta ratukamalla q'ipikunata saqiyukuykiman kaypi?

May I cross your property?
    chahk·*rai*·kekh keen·rai·*lyahn*·tah   *¿Chakraykiq*
    pah·sai·*mahn*·choo?   *kinrayllanta pasaymanchu?*
Can we go through here?
    kai·*neen*·tah   *¿Kayninta*
    poo·ree·koo·*mahn*·choo?   *puriykumanchu?*
Is this water OK to drink?
    ah·*lyeen*·choo   *¿Allinchu*
    ook·yah·*nah*·pahkh kai *oo*·noo?   *ukyanapaq kay unu?*
I'm lost.
    cheen·*kahs*·kahn poo·ree·*shah*·nee   *Chinkasqan purishani.*

altitude	*sah*·yai	sayay
altitude sickness	soo·*roo*·chee	suruchi
backpack	k'e·pee	q'ipi
candle	bee·lah	bila
to climb	wee·chai/*se*·kai	wichay/siqay
downhill	oo·rai	uray
first-aid kit	hahm·pee choo·*rah*·nah	hampi churana
gloves	wahn·tees	wantis
guide	poo·sahkh	pusaq
guided trek	poo·*sahkh*·wahn poo·ree	pusaqwan puriy
hike/to hike	poo·ree	puriy
hunting	chah·koo	chaku
hut	ch'ookh·lyah	ch'uklla
lookout	k-hah·*wah*·nah	qhawana
map	mah·pah	mapa
mountain climbing	or·ko wee·chai	urqu wichay
pick (tool)	pee·koo	piku
provisions (food)	ko·kow	quqaw
provisions (things)	kahkh·*koo*·nah	kaqkuna
rock climbing	kah·kah wee·chai	qaqa wichay
rope	wahs·k-hah	waskha
signpost	oo·*nahn*·chah	unancha
steep	sah·yahkh	sayaq
trek/to trek	kah·roo poo·ree	karu puriy
uphill	wee·chai/*hah*·nai	wichay/hanay
to walk	poo·ree	puriy

CAMPING   **KARPA RUWAY**

Designated camp sites exist only in tourist places like Machu Picchu or Sacsayhuamán. As long as you have permission from the locals, you can pitch your tent almost anywhere.

Is there a camp site nearby?
  kahn·choo kai·pee pahm·pah   ¿Kanchu kaypi pampa
  kahr·pah·pahkh?   karpapaq?
Can we camp here?
  kahr·pah·tah   ¿Karpata
  roo·wai·koo·mahn·choo   ruwaykumanchu
  kai·pee?   kaypi?
Who owns this land?
  pekh·tahkh kai chahkh·rah?   ¿Piqtaq kay chakra?
Can I talk to him/her?
  ree·mai·mahn·choo pai·wahn?   ¿Rimaymanchu paywan?
Where can I hire a tent?
  mai·pee·tahkh kahr·pah·tah   ¿Maypitaq karpata
  ahl·kee·lah·rui·mahn?   alkilarquyman?
Are there shower facilities?
  kahn·choo bah·nyoo   ¿Kanchu bañu
  ahr·mah·koo·nah·pahkh?   armakunapaq?

blanket	*choo·see/kah·tah/* *mahn·tah*	*chusi/qata/* *manta*
camping	kahm·pah·*meen*·too	*kampamintu*
camp site	kahr·*pah*·pahkh *pahm*·pah	*karpapaq* *pampa*
firewood	*lyahn*·t'ah	*llant'a*
hammer	tah·*kah*·nah	*takana*
hammock	ah·*mah*·kah	*amaka*
knife	koo·*chee*·lyoo/ koo·*choo*·nah	*kuchillu/* *kuchuna*
matches	p·hoos·*poo*·roo	*phuspuru*
mattress (bedding)	poo·*nyoo*·nah	*puñuna*
rope	*wahs*·k·hah	*waskha*
sleeping bag	poo·*nyoo*·nah	*puñuna*
tent (pegs)	*kahr*·pah (tah·kahr·poo·*koo*·nah)	*karpa* *(takarpukuna)*
torch (flashlight)	k'ahn·*chah*·nah/ leen·*teer*·nah	*k'anchana/* *lintirna*
water	*oo*·noo/*yah*·koo	*unu/yaku*
water bottle	woo·*tee*·lyah *oo*·noo/*yah*·koo	*wutilla* *unu/yaku*

WEATHER

PACHA/TIMPU

What's the weather like?
ee·*mai*·nahn *pah*·chah/
teem·poo *kah*·shahn?

¿Imaynan pacha/
timpu kashan?

What's the forecast for tomorrow?
ee·*mai*·nahn *pah*·chah/
teem·poo *kahn*·kah
pah·*kah*·reen?

¿Imaynan pacha/
timpu kanqa
paqarin?

Today it's ...	...shahn *koo*·nahn *p'oon*·chai	...-shan kunan p'unchay.
cold/chilly	*chee*·ree	*chiri*
hot/sunny	*roo*·p·hah	*rupha*
windy	*seen*·chee *wai*·rah	*sinchi wayra*

TREKKING

TREKKING

It's raining heavily.
nee·*shoo*·tahn pah·*rah*·shahn   *Nishutan parashan.*
It's raining lightly.
pee·see·*lyah*·tahn pah·*rah*·shahn   *Pisillatan parashan.*
It's flooding.
lyok·lyah·*shahn*·mee   *Lluqllashanmi.*

cloud	p-hoo·yoo	phuyu
dew	ch-hoo·lyah	chhulla
drizzle	ee·p-hoo	iphu
dry season	ch'ah·kee mee·tah	ch'aki mita
fog/mist	pah·chah p-hoo·yoo	pacha phuyu
frost	kah·sah/k-hoo·pah	qasa/qhupa
glacier	ree·t'ee	rit'i
hail	cheek·chee	chikchi
hot	roo·p-hoo	rupha
ice	ch-hoo·lyoon·koo	chhullunku
lightning	ee·lyah·pah/ lyeef·lyee	illapa/ lliphlli
rain	pah·rah	para
rainy season	pah·rai mee·tah	paray mita
shade	lyahn·t-hoo	llanthu
snow	ree·t'ee	rit'i
storm	lyokh·lyah pah·rah	lluqlla para
sun	een·tee	inti
sunny	roo·p-hah	rupha
thunder	k-hahkh·yah	qhaqya
warm	toom·pah·lyah·tah roo·p-hah	tumpallata rupha
wind	wai·rah	wayra
windy	seen·chee wai·rah	sinchi wayra

GEOGRAPHICAL TERMS

PACHA SUTIKUNA

cave	*mah*·ch'ai	mach'ay
cliff	*kah*·kah	qaqa
earthquake	*pah*·chah *koo*·yui	pacha kuyu
forest	*mahly*·kee *mahly*·kee	mallki mallki
gap	*k'eekh*·lyoo	k'ikllu
high plateau	*poo*·nah/*sahly*·kah	puna/sallqa
hill	or·*ko*·chah/*mo*·ko	urqucha/muqu
hot spring	*k'o*·nee *pook*·yoo	q'uñi pukyu
hot valley	*yoon*·kah	yunka
lake	*ko*·chah	qucha
mountain	or·ko	urqu
mountain path	or·*ko*·pee nyahn	urqupi ñan
pass (narrow)	*k'ah*·sah	q'asa
peak	or·kohk *poon*·tahn	urquq puntan
ravine	*wai*·k'o	wayq'u
river	*mah*·yoo	mayu
sea	ko·chah·*mah*·mah	quchamama
snow line	*ree*·t'ee *se*·ke	rit'i siqi
stone/rock	*roo*·mee/*wahn*·k'ah	rumi/wank'a
volcano	*nee*·nah p-*hokh*·chekh	nina phuqchiq
	or·ko	urqu
waterfall	p-*hahkh*·chah/p-*how*·chee	phaqcha/phawchi

TREKKING

FAUNA

What animal is that?

ee·mah ah·nee·*mahl*·tahkh chai?

IMAYMANA ANIMALKUNA

¿Ima animaltaq chay?

Domestic Creatures

alpaca	ahl·*pah*·kah	alpaka
cat	mee·see/mee·chee	misi/michi
dog	*ahl*·ko/aly·ko	alqu/allqu
donkey	*ahs*·noo	asnu
goat	kow·rah	kawra
horse	kah·*wah*·lyoo	kawallu
guanaco (like a llama)	wah·*nah*·koo	wanaku
llama	*lyah*·mah	llama
mule	moo·lah	mula
ox	*too*·roo	turu
pig	k·*hoo*·chee	khuchi
sheep	*ook*·yah/oo·*wee*·hah	ukya/uwiha

Uywakuna

Birds

Andean flamingo	pah·ree·*wah*·nah	pariwana
Andean songbird	*poo*·kui *poo*·kui	pukuy pukuy
condor	*koon*·toor	kuntur
wild duck	*choo*·lyoo *mah*·yoo	chullu mayu
eagle	*ahn*·kah	anka
falcon/hawk	*wah*·mahn	waman
hummingbird	(ko·ree) *k'en*·tee	(quri) q'inti
owl	*too*·koo/*hoo*·koo	tuku/huku
partridge	*yoo*·t·hoo/*lyoo*·t·hoo	yuthu/lluthu
rooster	*k'ahn*·kah	k'anka
seagull	*kely*·wah/*kyoo*·lyah/ kely·*wai*·too	qillwa/qiwlla/ qillwaytu
sparrowhawk	*ahn*·kah/*wah*·mahn	anka/waman
turtledove	*kooly*·koo	kullku
vulture	soo·we·*k'ah*·rah	suwiq'ara
woodpecker	hah·*k'ahkh*·lyoo	hak'akllu

Pisqukuna

TREKKING

Wildlife   Salqa Animalkuna

armadillo	keer·*keen*·choo	*kirkinchu*
bear	oo·*koo*·koo	*ukuku*
deer	tah·*roo*·kah	*taruka*
fish	*chahly*·wah	*challwa*
fox	*ah*·tokh	*atuq*
frog	hahm·*p'ah*·too	*hamp'atu*
game (animals)	chah·koo·*nah*·pahkh	*chakunapaq*
	ah·nee·mahl·*koo*·nah	*animalkuna*
leech	*yah*·wahr *ch'on*·kahkh	*yawar ch'unqaq*
lizard	soo·koo·*lyoo*·koo/	*sukulluku/*
	kah·*rai*·wah	*qaraywa*
monkey	koo·*see*·lyoo	*kusillu*
mountain lion	*poo*·mah	*puma*
snake	mah·*ch'ahkh*·wai/	*mach'aqway/*
	ah·*mah*·roo	*amaru*
spider	ah·*rah*·nyah;	*araña;*
	koo·see·*koo*·see	*kusi-kusi*
trout	*troo*·chah	*trucha*
turtle	chah·*rah*·pah	*charapa*
vicuña	wee·*k'oo*·nyah	*wik'uña*
(like a llama)		
viscacha (rodent)	wees·*k'ah*·chah	*wisk'acha*
wildcat	os·*k·ho*·lyoo	*usqhullu*
wild pig	see·*wai*·roo	*siwayru*

Insects   Kuru

bee	lah·*chee*·wah	*lachiwa*
butterfly	peely·*peen*·too	*pillpintu*
cockroach	koo·kah·*rah*·chah	*kukaracha*
dung beetle	*ah*·kah *tahn*·kah	*aka tanqa*
flea	*pee*·kee	*piki*
fly	*ch'oos*·pee	*ch'uspi*
louse/lice	oo·sah/oo·sah·*koo*·nah	*usa/usakuna*
mosquito	*k·he*·te *(ch'oos*·pee)	*qhiti (ch'uspi)*

TREKKING

TREKKING

THE LEGEND OF THE INCAS

At the beginning of time, near Lake Titicaca high in the Peruvian Andes, in a place known as Paqariqtampu, pah·kah·rekh·*tahm*·poq there appeared four brothers and four sisters, who were all children of the Sun, the highest of deities. The Sun charged these brothers and sisters with teaching humankind the principles of civilization, truth and justice. For this purpose, he gave them a golden staff, with which they were to seek out the ideal site to found an empire. They would know this site when the staff was swallowed up completely by the earth, upon striking the ground.

The brothers and sisters began their search for an empire by first organising the people living around Paqariqtampu into *ayllus*, ai·lyoos, or communities. They taught the people to cultivate the land, weave fibres and build houses; about laws, wars and the religion of the Sun. After this, everyone departed in search of their promised land, and *Manqu Khapaq*, mahn·ko k·hah·pahkh, and *Mama Uqllu*, mah·mah okh·lyo, the principal figures of the divine family, struck the ground every day with the magic staff. Finally, they arrived near a hill called Wanakawri, wah·nah·kow·ree, where, with the first strike, the golden staff disappeared. *Manqu Khapaq* and *Mama Uqllu* decided to establish the city of Qusqu, kos·ko, or 'Cuzco', which became the centre of their empire, Tawantinsuyu, tah·wahn·teen·soo·yoq, meaning 'four parts or regions (of the empire)'.

FLORA & AGRICULTURE
Trees, Plants & Flowers

MALLKI MALLKIPAS CHAKRA RURUPAS
Sach'akunapas Yurakunapas

What ... is that?	*ee·mah ... chai?*	*¿Ima ... chay?*
tree	*sah·ch'ah·tahkh*	*sach'ataq*
plant	*yoo·rah·tahkh*	*yurataq*
flower	*t'ee·kah·tahkh*	*t'ikataq*
agave (aloe)	*pahkh·pah*	*paqpa*
broom (bush)	*t'ahn·kahr*	*t'anqar*
cactus	*k'ahkh·lyah/ ah·nyah·pahn·koo*	*k'aklla/ añapanku*
cactus fruit	*too·nahs*	*tunas*
coca	*koo·kah*	*kuka*
eucalyptus	*yoo·kah·leekh·too*	*yukaliptu*
medlar	*wees·wee·roo*	*wiswiru*
mountain grass	*ee·ch·hoo*	*ichhu*
nettle	*kee·sah/k'oo·rah*	*kisa/k'ura*
pine	*pee·noo*	*pinu*
quingual (Andean tree)	*keen·wahl*	*kinwal*
scrub	*ch'ah·p-hrah*	*ch'aphra*
thorn/spine	*kees·kah*	*kiska*
totora reed	*t'oo·too·rah*	*t'utura*
white poplar	*kees·wahr*	*kiswar*
wild cherry tree	*kah·poo·lee*	*kapuli*

Herbs & Crops

Qurakunapis, Rurukunapis

beans	*ahl·weer·hahs*	*alwirhas*
cabbage	*koo·lees*	*kulis*
coriander *(cilantro)*	*koo·lahn·troo*	*kulantru*
corn	*sah·rah*	*sara*
fava beans	*hah·wahs*	*hawas*
flower	*t'ee·kah/wai·tah*	*t'ika/wayta*

TREKKING

garlic	*ah*·hoos	*ahus*
huacatay (aromatic herb)	wah·*kah*·tai	*wakatay*
kiwicha (grain)	kee·*wee*·chah	*kiwicha*
leaf	*rah*·p-hee/*rah*·p'ah	*raphi/rap'a*
lemon tree	*lee*·moon *sah*·ch'ah	*limun sach'a*
lupine	*tahr*·wee	*tarwi*
mashua (local tuber)	*ah*·nyoo/*mahs*·wah	*añu/maswa*
oca (tuber)	o·kah	*uqa*
onion	see·*wee*·lyah	*siwilla*
orange tree	lah·*rahn*·hah *sah*·ch'ah	*laranha sach'a*
orchard	*moo*·yah	*muya*
papaya (highland)	pah·*pah*·yah	*papaya*
parsley	pee·*ree*·heel	*pirihil*
peas	ahl·*weer*·hahs	*alwirhas*
potatoes	*pah*·pah	*papa*
quinoa	*kyoo*·nah/*kyoo*·nyah	*kiwna/kiwña*
tree	*mahly*·kee	*mallki*
wheat	*tree*·yoo	*triyu*
yacón (tuber)	*lyah*·kom/*yah*·koo	*llaqum/yaku*

Use Quechua for building a rapport with market vendors.

LOOKING FOR ...   ... MASKHAY

Where's a/the nearest ...?	mai·*pee*·tahkh ... kahn?	¿Maypitaq ... kan?
bank	*kol*·ke *wah*·see	qulqi wasi
market	k-*hah*·too	qhatu
music shop	moo·*see*·kah teen·dah	musika tinda
pharmacy	hahm·*pee*·yokh *wah*·see	hampiyuq wasi
shoe shop	sah·*pah*·too teen·dah	sapatu tinda
shop	teen·dah	tinda

Where can I buy (a) ...?	mai·*pee*·tahkh ... rahn·tee·*rui*·mahn?	¿Maypitaq ... rantirquyman?
book	lyoo·roo·koo·*nah*·tah	liwrukunata
clothes	p'ah·chah·koo·*nah*·tah	p'achakunata
handicrafts	ahr·tee·sah·nee·yah·koo·*nah*·tah	artisaniyakunata
souvenirs	*too*·kui *reek*·ch'ahkh ee·mai·mah·nah·koo·*nah*·tah	tukuy rikch'aq imaymanakunata

Where can I get a haircut?	mai·*pee*·tahkh chook·*chai*·tah roo·too·chee·koo·*rui*·mahn?	¿Maypitaq chukchayta rutuchikurquyman?

MAKING A PURCHASE   RANTIY

I'd like to buy ...	...·tah rahn·*tee*·tahn moo·*nai*·mahn	...·ta rantiytan munayman.
I'm just looking.	k-hah·*wai*·lyahn k-hah·wah·*shah*·nee	Qhawayllan qhawashani.
Can you write down the price?	chah·*neen*·tah kel·kahn·kee·*mahn*·choo?	¿Chaninta qilqankimanchu?

Can I look at it?
k·hah·wai·kui·*mahn*·choo?   ¿*Qhawaykuymanchu?*

Do you have any others?
hokh·*koo*·nah   ¿*Huqkuna*
kah·poo·soon·*kee*·choo?   *kapusunkichu?*

I don't like it.
mah·nahn *kai*·tah   *Manan kayta*
moo·nah·*nee*·choo   *munanichu.*

OK, I'll buy it.
ah·*lyeen*,·mee *chai*·tah   *Allinmi, chayta*
ah·pah·*koo*·sahkh/   *apakusaq/rantisaq.*
rahn·*tee*·sahkh

How much is it all together?
hai·k'ahn lyoo·*neen*·koo? ¿*Hayk'an lliwninku?*

Could I have a receipt please?
ree·see·*woo*·tah   ¿*Risiwuta*
ko·wahn·kee·*mahm*·choo?   *quwankimanchu?*

I want to exchange this.
kai·tah kahm·bee·*yai*·tah *Kayta kambiyayta*
moo·*nah*·nee   *munani.*

It's faulty.
mah·nahn kai ah·*lyeen*·choo *Manan kay allinchu.*

I'd like my money back.
kol·*kee*·tah koo·tee·chee·*poo*·wai *Qulqiyta kutichipuway.*

THEY MAY SAY ...

yow *(tai*·tah *reen*·goo; *mah*·mah *reen*·gah)!
Listen (Sir/Madam)!

ee·mah·lyah·*tah*·pahs rahn·*tee*·wai, tai·*tai*/mah·*mai*
Please buy something from me, Sir/Madam.

hai·*k'ah*·tahn moo·*nahn*·kee?
How much/many do you want?

chah·*neen*·tah pee·see·yah·*chee*·sahkh *ree*·kee
I'll lower the price for you.

BARGAINING CHANINTA PISIYACHIY

Bargaining is a widespread practice in Latin America, especially in Peru. You can bargain for just about anything, except perhaps your bill at a fine restaurant or the cost of something at a department store. You'll definitely be expected to bargain with street or market sellers.

How much is this?
hai·*k'ah*·tahkh chai? ¿Hayk'ataq chay?

Really?
che·*kahkh*·choo? ¿Chiqaqchu?

The price is too high.
seen·chee chah·nee·*yokh*·mee chai Sinchi chaniyuqmi chay.

It's too much for me.
mah·nahn *kol*·kay Manan qulqiy
ai·pah·*wahn*·choo aypawanchu.

Can you lower the price?
chah·*neen*·tah ¿Chaninta
pee·see·yah·cheen·kee·*mahm*·choo/ pisiyachinkimanchu/
oo·rai·kah·cheen·kee·*mahn*·choo? uraykachinkimanchu?

Do you have something cheaper?
mah·nah *ahn*·chah chah·*nee*·yokh ¿Mana ancha chaniyuq
ee·mah·lyai·*kee*·pahs imallaykipas
kah·poo·soon·*kee*·choo? kapusunkichu?

Is that your final price?
chai·choo chah·*neen* *ree*·kee? ¿Chaychu chanin riki?

I'll give you ...
...·tah koy·koo·*sai*·kee ...-ta quykusayki.

SOUVENIRS IMAYMANAKUNA RANTINAPAQ

baskets	ai·sah·nah·*koo*·nah/	aysanakuna/
	p'ookh·too·*koo*·nah/	p'uktukuna/
	kah·nahs·tah·*koo*·nah	kanastakuna
handicrafts	ahr·tee·sah·nee·yah·*koo*·nah	artisaniyakuna
jewellery	ee·*lyah*/oo·*mee*·nyah	illa/umiña

masks	oo·yah·tee·*koo*·nah	*uyatikuna*
musical	moo·*see*·kah	*musika*
instruments	wah·kah·chee·nah·*koo*·nah	*waqachinakuna*
pottery	*rahkh*·chee/*k'ahkh*·rah	*raqchi/k'akra*
shell souvenirs	ch'oo·roo·*mahn*·tah	*ch'urumanta*
	roo·*wahs*·kah	*ruwasqa*
	ee·mah·mai·nah·*koo*·nah	*imamaynakuna*
tapestries	t'e·ke·*koo*·nah	*t'iqikuna*
wood carvings	k'oo·lyoo·*mahn*·tah	*k'ullumanta*
	roo·*wahs*·kah	*ruwasqa*
	reekh·ch'ay	*rikch'ay*
woven textiles	ah·wai·*koo*·nah	*awaykuna*

CLOTHING   P'ACHA

bag	wah·*yah*·kah	*wayaqa*
belt (Andean)	*choom*·pee	*chumpi*
blanket	*kah*·tah/*choo*·see/	*qata/chusi/*
boots	*boo*·tahs	*butas*
cap (Andean)	ch'oo·lyoo	*ch'ullu*
dress	*p'ah*·chah	*p'acha*
handbag	ch'oos·pah	*ch'uspa*
hat	soom·*ree*·roo	*sumriru*
jacket	*sah*·koo	*saku*
jeans	pahn·*tah*·loon	*pantalun*
jumper (sweater)	*choom*·pah	*chumpa*
poncho	*poon*·choo	*punchu*
purse	ch'oos·pah	*ch'uspa*
scarf	chah·*lee*·nah	*chalina*
shawl	*lyeekh*·lyah	*lliklla*
shirt	kah·*mee*·sah	*kamisa*
shoes	sah·pah·too·*koo*·nah	*sapatukuna*
skirt	poo·*lyee*·rah	*pullira*
socks	*mee*·dyahs	*midyas*
T-shirt	*oon*·k·hoo/	*unkhu/*
	kah·mee·*see*·tah	*kamisita*

Can I try it on?
  choo·rah·kui·koo·*mahn*·choo *chai*·tah?
It doesn't fit.
  mah·nahn sah·yai·*nee*·choo

  ¿*Churakuykumanchu chayta?*

  Manan sayayniychu.

It's too ...	*kai*·kah ...mee/-n	Kayqa ...-mi/-n.
big	*hah*·toon	hatun
large	*seen*·chee *hah*·toon	sinchi hatun
long	*wahs*·k'ah	wask'a
small	*hoo*·chui	huchuy
short	*teen*·koo/*tahkh*·sah	tinku/taksa
tight	*k'ees*·kee	k'iski

MATERIALS   IMATAPAS RUWANAPAQ

bamboo	to·*ko*·ro/*so*·kos	tuquru/suqus
bone	too·lyoo	tullu
ceramic	*rahkh*·chee/*k'ahkh*·rah	raqch'i/k'akra
clay	*lyahn*·k'ee/*lyeen*·k'ee	llank'i/llink'i
cotton	*oot*·k·hoo	utkhu
handmade	mah·*kee*·wahn	makiwan
	roo·*wahs*·kah	ruwasqa
fabric	*lyee*·kah/*ah*·wah	llika/awa
glass	*kes*·pee	qispi
gold	*ko*·ree	quri
horn	*wahkh*·rah	waqra
leather	*kah*·rah	qara
metal	*ahn*·tah/*tee*·tee	anta/titi
plastic	plahs·*tee*·koo	plastiku
reed	*so*·kos/*k'oor*·koor	suqus/k'urkur
silver	*kol*·ke	qulqi
stainless steel	ah·*see*·roo	asiru
stone	*roo*·mee	rumi
straw	*ee*·ch·hoo	ichhu
thread	*k'ai*·too	q'aytu
wood	*k'oo*·lyoo	k'ullu
wool	*meely*·mah/*meely*·wah	millma/millwa

SHOPPING

COLOURS

		LLIMP'IKUNA
black	*yah·*nah	*yana*
blue	*ahn·*kahs/*ah·*sool	*anqas/asul*
brown	*ch'oom·*pee	*ch'umpi*
colour	*lyeem·*p'ee/*koo·*loor/	*llimp'i/kulur/*
	*tooly·*pee	*tullpi*
green	*k'o·*mer	*q'umir*
grey	*o·*kel/*ch'ekh·*chee/*tee·*tee	*uqi/ch'iqchi/titi*
orange	*wee·lah·*pee	*wilapi*
pink	*pahn·*tee;	*panti;*
	*lyahn·*k-hah *poo·*kah	*llanqha puka*
purple	*koo·*lyee/*moo·rah·*roo	*kulli/muraru*
red	*poo·*kah	*puka*
white	*yoo·*rahkh	*yuraq*
yellow	*k'e·*lyoo	*q'illu*

WOOLLY LOGIC

In the Andes, several wool-producing animals have been domesticated and are clipped for their wool. These include alpacas *(alpaka,* ahl·*pah·*kah*)*, guanacos *(wanaku,* wah·*nah·*koo*)*, sheep *(ukya/uwiha,* ook·*yah/oo·wee·*hah*)* and llamas *(llama,* lyah·*mah).* The alpaca-like vicuña *(wik'uña,* wee·*k'oo·*nyah*)*, an undomesticated species, was once hunted for its wool, but it's now considered endangered. No matter what its source, the word for wool in Quechua is *millma,* meely·mah, or its variant, *millwa,* meely·wah.

Wool can be used to make a range of clothing and accessories which traditionally exhibit a variety of regional motifs *(pallay,* pah·lyai*)*. Common designs include coca and potato flowers, llamas, alpacas and vicuñas, mountains, cacti, the Inca figure, masks, patterns of multi-coloured lines, birds, and silhouettes of towns and people working or socialising.

SHOPPING

TOILETRIES — SUMAQYACHIQKUNA

comb	nyahkh·ch'ah	ñaqch'a
razor	soon·k-hah roo·too·nah/ k'ee·soo·nah	sunkha rutuna/ k'isuna
shampoo	chahm·poo	champu
soap	hah·woon	hawun
tissues	sen·kah pee·chah·nah	sinqa pichana
toothbrush	kee·roo k-he·too·nah	kiru qhituna

FOR THE BABY — WAWACHAPAQ

baby powder	wah·wah·pahkh tahl·koo	wawapaq talku
bib	bah·bee·roo	babiru
bottle	bee·bee·roon	bibirun
nappies/diapers	ah·kah·wah·rah/ wahl·t'ah·nah	akawara/ walt'ana
dummy/pacifier	nyoo·nyoo·nah	ñuñuna
teat	nyoo·nyoo	ñuñu

SMOKING — PITAY

Smoking is much more common among men than women; traditionally, it's unacceptable for women to smoke. As times have changed, some women have taken it up, especially the *hampiq*, *hahm*·pekh, or folk healers. You should ask if it's OK to light up when in close proximity to others.

Do you sell cigarettes here?
see·yah·roo·koo·*nah*·tah been·deen·*kee*·choo? — ¿Siyarukunata bindinkichu?

Do you smoke?
pee·tahn·*kee*·choo kahn? — ¿Pitankichu qan?

Do you have a light?
foos·poo·*rui*·kee *kahn*·choo? — ¿Phuspuruyki kanchu?

Do you mind if I smoke?
pee·tai·*mahn*·choo kai·pee? — ¿Pitaymanchu kaypi?

Please don't smoke.
ah·*lyee*·choo ah·mah pee·*tai*·choo — Allichu ama pitaychu.

cigarettes	see·*yah*·roo	*siyaru*
cigars	*hah*·toon ch'oom·pee	*hatun ch'umpi*
	see·*yah*·roo	*siyaru*
lighter	*nee*·nah rah·tah·*chee*·nah;	*nina ratachina;*
	k'ahn·chah·*chee*·nah	*k'anchachina*
matches	foos·*poo*·roo	*phuspuru*
tobacco	tah·*wah*·koo	*tawaku*

SIZES & COMPARISONS
SAYAYKUNAPAS TINKUCHIKUYKUNAPAS

a little bit	pee·see·*lyah*·tah/	*pisillata/*
	toom·pah·*lyah*·tah	*tumpallata*
also	....pees/·pahs	*...-pis/-pas*
big	*hah*·toon	*hatun*
enough	chai·*lyah*·nyah	*chayllaña*
heavy	*lyah*·sahkh	*llasaq*
light	ch-*hah*·lyah	*chhalla*
little (amount)	*pee*·see/*toom*·pah	*pisi/tumpa*
many	*ahs*·k·hah/*ch-hee*·kah	*askha/chhika*
more	*ahs*·wahn	*aswan*
small	*hoo*·chui	*huchuy*
too much/ many	*ahs*·k·hah *ahs*·k·hah; *ch-hee*·kah *ch-hee*·kah	*askha askha; chhika chhika*

A great variety of dishes and cuisine is available throughout the Andes. In most restaurants, staff will speak Spanish, so Quechua will be more useful for visits to local markets, fairs, festivals and small restaurants.

THROUGH THE DAY   P'UNCHAYNINTIN

Since rural Andeans rise with the sun, breakfast may be as early as five or six o'clock in the morning. Lunch, the biggest meal of the day, is at midday, while dinner is around six in the evening. Bedtime is generally at nightfall. This routine varies for festivals and holidays, when everyone has a chance to party.

breakfast	*mah·*tee; *oo·*noo *k'o·*nyee	*mati; unu q'uñi*
lunch	ahl·*moo·*sai/*mee·*k-hui	*almusay/mikhuy*
dinner	*too·*tah *mee·*k-hui; *see·*nah	*tuta mikhuy; sina*

SPECIAL DIETS   QHALI KAYPAQ MIKHUYKUNA

Meat is an integral part of the Andean diet, even though it may be served in small quantities. You won't find vegetarian meals in small rural restaurants or when staying at someone's home.

Does this dish have meat in it?
    ai·chah·*yokh·*choo kai
    mee·*k-hoo·*nah?
                ¿Aychayuqchu kay
                mikhuna?

Can I get this without meat?
    *mah·*nah ai·chah·*yohkh·*tah
    kah·rai·koo·wahn·kee·*mahn·*choo
    *kai·*tah?
                ¿Mana aychayuqta
                qaraykuwankimanchu
                kayta?

I don't eat meat.
mah·nahn ai·*chah*·tah   Manan aychata
mee·k·hoo·*nee*·choo   mikhunichu.

I don't eat chicken or fish.
mah·nahn *wahly*·pah ai·*chah*·tah,   Manan wallpa aychata,
chahly·wah ai·*chah*·tah   challwa aychata
mee·*k·hoo*·*nee*·choo   mikhunichu.

I can't eat dairy products.
mah·nah lee·chee·*mahn*·tah   Manan lichimanta
roo·*wahs*·kah   ruwasqa
mee·k·hui·koo·*nah*·tah   mikhuykunata
mee·*k·hui*·tah ah·tee·*nee*·choo   mikhuyta atinichu.

Does it contain egg?
roon·too·*yohkh*·choo kai·kah?   ¿Runtuyuqchu kayqa?

I'm allergic to (peanuts).
mah·nahn (mah·*nee*)·tah   Manan (mani)-ta
mee·k·hoo·*nee*·choo.   mikhunichu.
ah·leer·*hee*·koon kah·nee   Alirhikun kani.

EATING OUT

MIKHUNA WASIPIPAS KARPAPIPAS MIKHUY

Eating out in rural areas means eating communally outdoors
during festivals, fairs or Sunday market days. Local dishes are
easily found in *chicherías*, or *chicha* bars – *aqha wasikuna,*
ah·khah wah·see·*koo*·nah – and *picanterías,* inexpensive
restaurants specialising in spicy dishes. For particularly spicy
food, try dishes labelled *arequipeña*, 'Arequipa style', or *a la
criolla*, 'Creole style'.

Is there anything to eat?
kahn·choo ee·mah·*lyah*·pahs   ¿Kanchu imallapas
mee·k·hoo·*nah*·pahk?   mikhunapaq?

Yes, there is.
ah·*ree, kahn*·mee   Arí, kanmi.

No, there isn't.
mah·nahn *kahn*·choo   Manan kanchu.

FOOD

Could you recommend something?
ee·mah·*tah*·tahkh
mee·k·hoo·*rui*·mahn?

¿Imatataq
mikhurquyman?

Is there any salad?
een·sah·*lah*·dah kahn·choo?

¿Insalada kanchu?

I'll have what they're having.
pai·*koo*·nah
mee·k·hoo·shahn·*koo*·tah
no·*kah*·pahs moo·*nah*·nee

Paykuna
mikhushankuta
nuqapas munani.

What's in that dish?
ee·mah·*yokh*·mee chai
mee·*k·hoo*·nah?

¿Imayuqmi chay
mikhuna?

COMPLIMENTS TO THE CHEF

I love this dish.
kai mee·k·hoo·*nah*·tah
ahn·*chah*·tah moo·*nah*·nee

Kay mikhunata
anchata munani.

I'm satisfied/full.
sahkh·*sahs*·kah kah·nee

Saksasqa kani.

We love the local cuisine.
kai lyahkh·*tah*·pee
mee·k·hoo·*nah*·tah
seen·*chee*·tah moo·*nai*·koo

Kay llaqtapi
mikhunata
sinchita munayku.

That was delicious!
soo·mahkh mee·*k·hoo*·nah!

¡Sumaq mikhuna!

You're an excellent cook.
koo·sah wai·*k'okh*·mee
kahn·kee

Kusa wayk'uqmi
kanki.

FOOD

I want cold/hot water please.
ah·*lyee*·choo *chee·ree/k'o*·nyee
oo·*noo*·tah moo·*nah*·nee

Allichu chiri/q'uñi
unuta munani.

May I have some more please?
ah·*lyee*·choo
yah·pah·yoo·wahn·*kee*·mahn

Allichu
yapayuwankiman.

Please give	ah·*lyee*·choo ....tah	*Allichu ...-ta*
me a/an/the ...	ko·wai	*quway.*
ashtray	*oosh*·pah choo·*rah*·nah	*ushpa churana*
bill	*kween*·tah	*kwinta*
cup	*sui*·k'oo/	*suyk'u/*
	chui·*k'oo*·chah/	*chuyk'ucha/*
	poo·koo	*puku*
fork	tee·*nee*·roor	*tinirur*
knife	koo·*chee*·lyoo	*kuchillu*
plate	*p'oo*·koo/*p'oo·koo*·chah	*p'uku/p'ukucha*
pot	*mahn*·kah	*manka*
spoon	koo·*chah*·rah	*kuchara*
water	oo·noo/*yah*·koo	*unu/yaku*
to boil	t'eem·*poo*·chee	*t'impuchiy*
boiled	t'eem·*poos*·kah	*t'impusqa*
bread (stale)	choo·choo *t'ahn*·tah	*chuchu t'anta*
clean (things)	leem·*pee*·yoo/*lui*·loo	*limpiyu/luylu*
clean (water)	*ch'oo*·yah	*ch'uya*
cold	*chee*·ree	*chiri*
to cook	*wai*·k'ui	*wayk'uy*
cooked	chah·*yahs*·kah	*chayasqa*

dirty	k·he·lyee/k·hahr·kah	qhilli/kharka
fresh (vegetables)	lyan·lyah	llanlla
greasy/fatty	wee·rah·sah·pah	wirasapa
to heat	k'o·nyee·chee	q'uñichiy
hot (temperature)	k'o·nyee	q'uñi
increase/addition	yah·pah	yapa
meat	(see k'ah) ai·chah	(siq'a) aycha
raw	hahn·kool/chah·wah	hanku/chawa
to salt	kah·chee·chai	kachichay
salty	kah·chee·sah·pah	kachisapa
sour	p'os·ko	p'usqu
spicy	hah·yah	haya
stale/spoiled	mah·k'ah	maq'a
sweet	mees·k'ee	misk'i
to sweeten	mees·k'ee·chee	misk'ichiy
tart	k·hahkh·teel/lyo·ke	qhaqti/lluqi
to taste	mah·lyee	malliy
thick	t·hah·kah	thaka
watery	yah·koo·sah·pah	yakusapa

ANDEAN COOK-OUTS

In many rural regions, midday meals for special occasions and celebrations are still prepared in a cooking pit, or *pachamanca*, pah·chah·*mahn*·kah. A hole is dug and a small 'house' of stones constructed over it. A fire is built inside the 'house', heating the stones until they're white-hot, at which point they're tumbled into the hole. Meats, tubers, vegetables, tamales (meat parcels), grains and herbs are sandwiched between the layers of hot rock. Finally, the oven is sealed shut with herbs and large leaves to keep soil from falling through into the food, and covered with earth to seal in the heat until it's cooked to perfection. Meals are served sitting in a circle on the ground and are eaten as finger food.

ANDEAN STAPLE DISHES   LLAQTANCHISPA MIKHUNAN

These are typical dishes that tend to be served every day, with little variation. Each region has its specialities but some dishes are common throughout the Andes:

chokh·lyo wai·k'oo *chuqllu wayk'u*
corn on the cob – available from March through to May, it's boiled and served with a kind of unripened cheese

choo·pee *chupi*
soup made from a variety of regional ingredients

ch'oo·nyoo *ch'uñu*
dried potatoes, *ch'arki*, *ch'ahr·kee*, and dried meat – similar to jerky – prepared with aromatic herbs

hah·k'oo/mahch·kah *hak'u/machka*
a flour made of any of a variety of grains (wheat, barley, quinoa or *cañihua*; or dried beans or peas)

hahn·k'ah/hahm·kah/ kahm·chah *hank'a/hamka/kamcha*
popcorn made from large kernels and served with a dry, cheddar-like cheese. The corn is toasted – or 'popped' – inside a *k'allana*, *k'ah·lyah·nah*, a low, open clay pot, and is put inside a clay oven known as a *q'uncha*, *k'on·chah*, or *tullpa*, *tooly·pah*.

moo·tee *mut'i*
dried corn kernels, boiled. A part of every corn harvest is set aside for drying, to be added to soup or ground into flour.

oo·choo koo·tah *uchu kuta*
hot pepper paste, that accompanies varieties of tuber

p-hoos·poo/poos·poo *phuspu/puspu*
dried beans (though can be fresh in season) reconstituted by boiling. All boiled foods are prepared in a clay pot known as a *manka*, *mahn·kah*.

FOOD

FOOD

REGIONAL SPECIALITIES   WAKIN LLAQTAKUNAQ MIKHUNAN

Note the Spanish influence in the names of many dishes.

Argentina

em·pah·*nah*·dahs   *empanadas* (Spanish)
   puff pastries filled with minced meat and spices and
   other ingredients served with *ruqru*, rokh·roo, a stew

Bolivia

ch'oo·nyoo   *ch'uñu*
   freeze-dried potatoes, soaked overnight and then
   boiled to accompany main dishes

em·pah·*nah*·dahs   *empanadas salteñas* (Spanish)
sahl·*te*·nyahs
   a type of meat pie

hahly·pah·*wai*·kah   *hallpawayka*
   sauce made from tomatoes, fresh peppers and herbs

pe·*kah*·nah   *pecana* (Spanish)
   traditional Christmas dish of beef or veal cooked in
   wine and herbs

pee·ke mah·cho   *pique macho* (Spanish)
   beef grilled with hot peppers, chopped potatoes and
   onions and served with fried potatoes and gravy, or
   with *saqta de pollo*

sahkh·tah de po·lyo   *saqta de pollo*
   chicken stew with peppers and onions

seel·*pahn*·cho   *silpancho cochabambino*
co·chah·bahm·*bee*·no
   meat and egg dish covered with hot sauce

teem·poo   *timpu*
   lamb stew

troo·chah   *trucha*
   trout, a Lake Titicaca speciality

toon·tah   *tunta*
   a type of freeze-dried potato, paler than the *ch'uñu*

Colombia

hoo·*meen*·t'ah   *humint'a*
   pork, vegetable and rice tamale, wrapped in banana
   leaves and steamed

ko·wee   *quwi*
   grilled guinea pig

Ecuador

cahl·do de *pah*·tahs   *caldo de patas* (Spanish)
   soup made with cow hooves

se·*vee*·che de cah·mah·*ron*   *ceviche de camarón*
   a type of shrimp cocktail   (Spanish)

free·*tah*·dah   *fritada* (Spanish)
   small pieces of fried pork, served with *muti*, fried
   bananas, potatoes and hot peppers

lyah·peen·*gah*·choo   *llapingacho*
   potato-based dish, like a potato pancake

lo·cro de *pah*·pah   *locro de papa*
   potato and cheese soup

po·lyo seen *po*·lyo   *pollo sin pollo* (Spanish)
   'chicken without chicken', a vegetarian dish common
   to Quito, Otavalo and Baños

se·co de *chee*·vo   *seco de chivo* (Spanish)
   goat stew served with rice

Peru

Ancash

hah·kah *chahs*·kee   *haka chaski*
   guinea pig soup

pah·pah *chahs*·kee   *papa chaski*
   potato soup made with milk and cottage cheese

pe·*cahn cahl*·do   *pecán caldo* (Spanish)
   lamb's head broth

roo·roo *hee*·lyee   *ruru hilli*
   fruit punch made with local seasonal fruits

FOOD

*wahly·*pah *chahs·*kee   *wallpa chaski*
  chicken broth with peanuts and almonds
*yoo·*kah *shoo·*pee   *yuka shupi*
  low-fat soup served the morning after a late night

Arequipa

*choo·*pee de cah·mah·*ro·*nes   *chupi de camarones*
  prawn soup
*pahn·*kah oo·*choo*   *panka uchu*
  a special form of the ever-present ground hot pepper
ro·co·to re·*lye·*no   *rocoto relleno* (Spanish)
  a variety of stuffed hot peppers

Ayacucho

ah·*roo·*woo   *aruwu*
  meat stew (most often pork)
chee·*chah·*roo   *chicharu*
  fried shredded pork and potatoes
*kahn·*kah   *kanka*
  roast beef sauteed with onions, garlic, hot peppers
  and spices
moon·*doon·*goo   *mundungu*
  thick, rich soup made with beef, lamb or pork, usually
  including the tripe
pah·*tah·*chee   *patachi*
  thick soup made with barley and bacon
poo·*chee·*roo/*teem·*poo   *puchiru/timpu*
  thick soup of varying meats, tubers, legumes and rice
*poo·*kah pee·*kahn·*tee   *puka pikanti*
  spicy stew based on potatoes, sugar beets and
  peanuts, usually served on rice
*ko·*wee *kahn·*kah   *quwi kanka*
  fried guinea pig

FOOD

Cuzco

chee·ree oo·choo *chiri uchu*
a spicy dish of fried meat and hot peppers, especially popular during the Corpus Christi festival

lo·mo *lomo* (Spanish)
fried beef prepared with onions, tomatoes, rice, potatoes, and a unique blend of seasonings

pah·ko·chah/ *paqucha/*
ahl·pah·kah ai·chah *alpaka aycha*
alpaca meat

pe·pyahn de kui *pepián de cuy* (Spanish)
fried rabbit or guinea pig served with rice and/or boiled potatoes

poo·chee·roo/teem·po *puchiru/timpu*
soup of steak, lamb's head, bacon and raisins, often including cabbage, potatoes, chickpeas and rice

troo·chah *trucha*
trout

Puno

kahn·kah·choo *kankachu*
roast suckling pig, veal or lamb, prepared with hot peppers, ground spices, white wine, lemon, garlic, oil and pureed papaya

kah·rah·chee teem·poo *karachi timpu*
thick fish stew made with *karachi,* kah·rah·chee (a fish from Lake Titicaca), *muña, moo·nyah* (an aromatic herb), *ch'uñu, ch'oo·nyoo,* garlic, onion and hot peppers

ke·so oo·mah·chah *queso umacha*
stew made with hot peppers, farmers' cheese, diced onion, milk and eggs, served over boiled potatoes

AT THE MARKET   QHATUPI

Where can I find the ...?
   mai·*pee*·tahkh ... kahn?   *¿Maypitaq ... kan?*
I want to buy some ...
   ...·tah rahn·*tee*·tah moo·*nah*·nee   *...-ta rantiyta munani.*

Meat & Poultry   Imaymana Aychakuna

beef	*wah*·kah *ai*·chah	*waka aycha*
chicken	*wahly*·pah *ai*·cha	*wallpa aycha*
dried meat/jerky	*ch'ahr*·kee	*ch'arki*
duck	*pah*·too *ai*·chah	*patu aycha*
eggs	*roon*·too	*runtu*
fat/grease	*wee*·rah	*wira*
goat	*kah*·brah *ai*·chah	*kabra aycha*
guinea pig	*ko·wee ai*·chah	*quwi aycha*
lamb	oo·*wee*·hah *ai*·chah	*uwiha aycha*
llama	*lyah*·mah *ai*·chah	*llama aycha*
meat	*ai*·chah	*aycha*
partridge	*lyoo*·t-hoo/	*lluthu/*
	yoo·too *ai*·chah	*yutu aycha*
pork	k-*hoo*·chee *ai*·chah	*khuchi aycha*
pork rind	k-*hoo*·chee *kah*·rahn	*khuchi qaran*
rabbit	*ko*·wee *ai*·chah	*quwi aycha*
ribs	*wahkh*·tah *ai*·chah	*waqta aycha*
tripe	*ch'oon*·chool	*ch'unchul*
turkey	*pah*·woo *ai*·chah	*pawu aycha*

Vegetables   Mikhuna Qurakuna

cabbage	*koo*·lees	*kulis*
capsicum	pee·*meen*·tah	*piminta*
carrot	sah·*noor*·yah	*sanurya*
corn kernels	wee·*nyah*·poo	*wiñapu*
corn (on the cob)	*chokh*·lyo ee·*lyah*·koo	*chuqllu illaku*
fava beans	*hah*·wahs	*hawas*
garlic	*ah*·hoos	*ahus*
hot pepper	ro·*ko*·to/*oo*·choo	*ruqutu/uchu*
lettuce	lee·*choo*·gah	*lichuga*

FOOD

onions (spring)	see·*wee*·lyah	*siwilla*
peas	ahl·*weer*·hahs	*alwirhas*
potato	*pah*·pah	*papa*
pumpkin	sah·*pah*·lyoo	*sapallu*
tomato	too·*mah*·tee	*tumati*

THE DIVINE POTATO

Andean legend relates that when the first Inca ruler *Manqu Khapaq* and his consort *Mama Uqllu* emerged from Lake Titicaca to found their empire, the first thing their god, *Wiraqucha*, wee·rah·*ko*·chah, did was to teach them to plant potato fields.

Andeans name new potato varieties in creative ways to reflect their shape, flavour and texture. The popular yellow potato is known as *runtu papa*, *roon*·too *pah*·pah; *runtu* is the Quechua word for 'egg', and this potato has similar qualities to a hard-boiled egg. Other names are equally evocative, such as the *yana ñawi*, *yah*·nah *nyah*·wee, or 'black-eyed potato', and the *q'uyu tawna*, *k'o*·yoo tow·nah, or 'purple walking cane'. There are nearly 4000 varieties of potato to be found in its place of origin, the Andes.

Pulses, Grains & Legumes Ch'aki Rurukuna

barley	see·*wah*·rah	*siwara*
bread	*t'ahn*·tah	*t'anta*
cañihua	kah·*nyee*·wah	*qañiwa*
dried beans	poo·*roo*·too	*purutu*
flour	*hah*·k'o	*hak'u*
kiwicha	kee·*wee*·chah	*kiwicha*
maize (dried corn)	*sah*·rah	*sara*
quinoa	kyoo·nyah/kyoo·nah	*kiwña/kiwna*
red and black bean	wai·*roo*·roo	*wayruru*
rice	*ah*·roos	*arus*
turnip (wild)	*yoo*·yoo	*yuyu*
wheat	*tree*·yoo	*triyu*

FOOD

Fruit

		Ruru
apple	mahn·*sah*·nah	*mansana*
avocado	*pahl*·tah	*palta*
banana	lah·*tah*·noos	*latanus*
fruit	*roo*·roo	*ruru*
medlar	nees·*pee*·roos/	*nispirus/*
(like crabapple)	wees·*wee*·roos	*wiswirus*
orange	lah·*rahn*·hah	*laranha*
peach	doo·*rahs*·noo	*durasnu*
sour cherry	kah·*poo*·lee/*reen*·dahs	*kapuli/rindas*
tumbo fruit	*teen*·teen	*tintin*

Dairy Products

		Lichimanta Mikhuykuna
butter	mahn·tee·*kee*·lyah	*mantikilla*
cheese	*kee*·soo	*kisu*
milk	*lee*·chee	*lichi*

Spices & Condiments

		Misk'ipakuna
chillies/hot pepper	*oo*·choo	*uchu*
cinnamon	kah·*nee*·lah	*kanila*
coriander *(cilantro)*	koo·*lahn*·troo	*kulantru*
garlic	*ah*·hoos	*ahus*
honey	lah·*chee*·wah/	*lachiwa/*
	ah·*nyah*·kah	*añaka*
huacatay	wah·*kah*·tai	*wakatay*
(aromatic herb)		
oil	ah·*see*·tee	*asiti*
parsley	pee·*ree*·heel	*pirihil*
pepper	pee·*meen*·tah	*piminta*
salt	*kah*·chee	*kachi*
sauce (of tomato	*oo*·choo koo·tah	*uchu kuta*
and hot pepper)		
sugar	*mees*·k'ee/ah·*soo*·kahr	*misk'i/asukar*

FOOD

DRINKS
Nonalcoholic

UKYANAKUNA
Ukyana

Every region has its typical fruit juices such as the *likwarus*, leek·wah·roos, 'fruit shakes', of Bolivia, widely available in cities. Soft drinks are rare but not impossible to find in rural areas, particularly during festivals and fairs. They're considered a great luxury for the highlanders, who usually drink herbal tea. One variety is *chicha (aqha/aha*, ah·k·hah/*ah·*hah, in Quechua) made from quinoa instead of corn.

chicha morada (made from purple corn)	koo·lyee *ah·*k-hah/*ah·*hah	*kulli aqha/aha*
coca leaf tea	koo·kah *mah·*tee	*kuka mati*
coffee	kah·fee	*kaphiy*
cold water	chee·ree oo·noo/*yah·*koo	*chiri unu/yaku*
corn tea (Bolivian)	ah·pee	*api*
(in Peru, *api* is purple cornstarch pudding)		
herbal tea	ko·rah oo·noo	*qura unu*
hot water	k'o·nyee oo·noo/*yah·*koo	*q'uñi unu/yaku*
juice	hee·lyee	*hilli*
lemonade	lee·moo·*nah·*rah	*limunara*
mineral water	woo·tee·*lyah·*pee oo·noo	*wutillapi unu*
soda/soft drink	koo·lah/gah·see·yoo·sah	*kula/gasiyusa*
tea ...	tee ...	*tiy ...*
with milk	lee·chee·*yokh·*tah	*lichiyuqta*
without milk	*mah·*nah lee·chee·*yokh·*tah	*mana lichiyuqta*
with sugar	mees·k'ee·*yokh·*tah; ah·soo·kahr·nee·*yokh·*tah	*misk'iyuqta asukarniyuqta*
without sugar	*mah·*nah mees·k'ee·*yokh·*tah; *mah·*nah ah·soo·kahr·nee·*yokh·*tah	*mana misk'iyuqta; mana asukarniyuqta*
toasted barley tea	see·*wah·*rah oo·noo	*siwara unu*
water	oo·noo/*yah·*koo	*unu/yaku*

FOOD

THE ANDEAN WONDER DRINK

The coca leaf has a long tradition of sacred and medicinal use in Andean cultures. It's most commonly chewed, or brewed as a tea, *kuka mati, koo·*kah *mah·*tee. The tea is prepared by pouring boiling water directly over the coca leaves, or by using coca tea bags which can be bought in any grocery store.

Coca's medicinal uses have been well documented. It's perhaps best known for its energising properties when one is hungry and tired, and for its ability to combat altitude sickness. Perhaps less well known by foreigners, but definitely appreciated by the locals, is its ability to aid digestion, cure diarrhoea and ease labour pains!

Alcoholic   Waqtu

Every region has its own special beers, wines and cocktails. Peru is known for *pisco, pees·*ko, a strong brandy distilled from grapes. *Chicha* or *aqha/aha, ah·*k-hah/*ah·*hah, is traditional corn beer, prepared and drunk throughout the Andean countries for centuries. *Singani*, seen·*gah·*nee, is a Bolivian drink made from a by-product of wine-making, mixed with lemon juice, lemon soda and ice.

beer	seer·*wee·*sah	*sirwisa*
brandy	*trah·*woo	*trawu*
chicha (maize beer)	*ah·*k-hah/*ah·*hah	*aqha/aha*
chicha bar	*ah·*k-hah *wah·*see	*aqha wasi*
singani	seen·*gah·*nee	*singani*

FOOD

Any health care in the high, remote Andes is likely to take place with a *hampiq*, hahm·pekh, 'healer' (or *curandero/a* (m/f) in Spanish), instead of a medical doctor. Healers use traditional folk medicine based on herbs, stones, potions and animal fats. Carry your own medicines or first aid kit with you when you're travelling, just to be on the safe side.

In metropolitan areas and populous regions, you'll always be able to find medical services. These places will operate in Spanish, as will the staff at the medical posts scattered few and far between in rural areas.

See Trekking, page 112, for advice on altitude sickness.

Is there a ...	*kahn·*choo ...	¿*Kanchu* ...
around here?	*kai·*pee?	*kaypi?*
chemist/ pharmacy	hahm·*pee·*yokh *wah·*see	*hampiyuq wasi*
dentist	*kee·*roo *see·*k'ekh	*kiru sik'iq*
doctor	mee·*dee·*kool*dook·*toor	*midiku/duktur*
healer	*hahm·*pekh	*hampiq*
hospital	hahm·*pee·*nah *wah·*see	*hampina wasi*

WITH THE HEALER   HAMPIQWAN

Could the healer come here?
    *pahkh·*tah hahm·*pekh·*kah   ¿*Paqta hampiqqa*
    *kai·*mahn hah·moo·*rui·*mahn?   *kayman hamurquyman?*
I'm sick.
    on·ko·*shah·*neen   *Unqushanin.*
My friend is sick.
    rekh·see·nah·kokh·*mah·*see   *Riqsinakuqmasiy*
    on·*ko·*shahn   *unqushan.*
I have a toothache.
    kee·*rui·*mee nah·nah·*wah·*shahn   *Kiruymi nanawashan.*

HEALTH

I've broken my tooth.
kee·*rui*·mee p'ah·*kee*·roon   *Kiruymi p'akirqun.*

My mouth hurts.
see·*mee*·mee nah·nah·*wah*·shahn   *Simiymi nanawashan.*

| Ouch! | ah·chah·*kow*! | ¡*Achakáw*! |

AILMENTS   UNQUYKUNA

I feel nauseous.
mee·lyah·nah·yah·wah·*shahn*·mee/   *Millanayawashanmi/*
wees·ch'oo·nah·yah·wah·*shahn*·mee   *Wisch'unayawashanmi.*

I feel under the weather.
mah·nahn ah·*lyeen*·choo   *Manan allinchu*
kah·*shah*·nee   *kashani.*

I feel weak.
mah·nah kahly·pah·*yokh*·mee   *Mana kallpayuqmi*
kah·*shah*·nee   *kashani.*

I'm ill.
on·ko·*shah*·neen   *Unqushanin.*

THE HEALER MAY SAY ...

ee·mah·nah·*soon*·keen?   ¿*Imanasunkin?*
   What's the matter?

ee·mai·lyai·*kee*·pahs   ¿*Imallaykipas*
nah·nah·soon·*kee*·choo?   *nanasunkichu?*
   Do you feel any pain?

mai·peen nah·nah·   ¿*Maypin nanasunki?*
soon·kee?
   Where does it hurt?

e·*mai*·keen nah·nah·   ¿*Imaykin nanasunki?*
soon·kee?
   What part of your body hurts?

HEALTH

THE HEALER MAY SAY ... (cont.)

roo·p-hai
on·koi·*wahn*·choo
kah·*shahn*·kee?
  *¿Ruphay
unquywanchu
kashanki?*
   Do you have a temperature?

hai·k'ah p'oon·*chai*·nyahn
on·ko·*shahn*·kee?
  *¿Hayk'a p'unchayñan
unqushanki?*
   How long have you been like this?

k'ee·koo·chee·koo·
shahn·*kee*·choo?;
yah·wahr·nee·*kee*·choo
hah·*moo*·shan?
  *¿K'ikuchikushankichu?;
¿Yawarniykichu
hamushan?*
   Are you menstruating?

week·sah·*yokh*·choo
kah·*shahn*·kee?
  *¿Wiksayuqchu
kashanki?*
   Are you pregnant?

kai *(k'o·*nyee) koo·kah
mah·*tee*·tah ook·yah·
kui·kui
  *Kay (q'uñi) kuka
matita ukyakuykuy.*
   Drink this cup of (hot) coca leaf tea.

no·kahn
hahm·pee·roo·*sai*·kee
  *Nuqan
hampirqusayki.*
   I'll cure your illness.

ah·mah lyah·kee·*kui*·choo,
koo·nah·chah·*lyahn*·mee
ah·lyeen·*yahn*·kee
  *Ama llakikuychu,
kunachallanmi
allinyanki.*
   Don't worry, you'll get well soon.

ah·*lyee*·choo ... *kai*·pee	*Allichu ...* *kaypi.*	Please ... here.
see·*ree*·kui	*sirikuy*	lie down
tee·*yah*·kui	*tiyakuy*	sit down
poo·*nyoo*·kui	*puñukuy*	sleep
sah·*mah*·kui	*samakuy*	rest

HEALTH

It hurts here.
    kai·pee nah·nah·*wah*·shahn

Kaypi nanawashan.

I feel better/worse.
    ah·lyeen·yah·*shah*·neen/
    seen·cheer·ko·*shah*·neen

Allinyashanin/
Sinchirqushanin.

I've been vomiting for (two days).
    (*ees*·kai p'oon·*chai*·nyahn)
    week·ch'oo·pah·*koo*·nee

(Iskay p'unchayñan)
wikch'upakuni.

I can't sleep.
    mah·nahn poo·*nyui*·tah
    ah·tee·*nee*·choo

Manan puñuyta
atinichu.

I burned myself.
    roo·p·hah·chee·koo·*roo*·neen

Ruphachikurqunin.

I've been bitten by a
dog/snake/insect.
    ahl·ko/mah·*ch'ahkh*·wai/
    koo·roo kah·nee·*roo*·wahn

Alqu/Mach'aqway/
Kuru kanirquwan.

I've sprained my wrist/ankle.
    mah·kee/*chah*·kee mo·*koy*·tahn
    k'e·wee·koo·*roo*·nee

Maki/Chaki muquytan
q'iwikurquni.

I think I have worms.
    week·*sai*·pee koo·roo·*yokh*·choos
    hee·nah kah·*shah*·nee

Wiksaypi kuruyuqchus
hina kashani.

I have a rash.
    k·*hee*·kee on·koy·*wahn*·mee
    kah·*shah*·nee

Khiki unquywanmi
kashani.

HEALTH

I feel ...	...*wahn*·mee kah·*shah*·nee	...-wanmi kashani.
dizzy	*oo*·mah *moo*·yui	uma muyuy
shivery	k-hah·*tah*·tai	khatatay

I have (a/an) ...	...*wahn*·mee kah·*shah*·nee	...-wanmi kashani.
altitude sickness	soo·*roo*·chee	suruchi
bronchitis	*nee*·shoo oo·hoo	nishu uhu
chickenpox	sah·rahn·*pee*·yoon	saranpiyun
cold	*chee*·ree on·koy	chiri unquy
constipation	*ah*·kah *k'ees*·kee	aka k'iski
cough	*oo*·hoo	uhu
diarrhoea	*k'e*·chah on·koy	q'icha unquy
fever	*roo*·p-hai on·koy	ruphay unquy
fleas	*pee*·kee	piki
headache	*oo*·mah *nah*·nai	uma nanay
influenza	*ch-hoo*·lyee/ *hah*·ch'ee	chhulli/ hach'i
lice	oo·sah·*koo*·nah	usakuna
lump	*k'om*·poo	q'umpu
malaria	*chookh*·choo on·koy	chukchu unquy
migraine	*nee*·shoo oo·mah *nah*·nai	nishu uma nanay
rash	k-*hee*·kee/k-*heer*·kee	khiki/khirki
sore throat	*ton*·kor *nah*·nai	tunqur nanay
stomachache	*week*·sah *nah*·nai	wiksa nanay
sunburn	*roo*·p-hai	ruphay
toothache	*kee*·roo *nah*·nai	kiru nanay
urinary tract infection	*hees*·p'ai *p'ee*·tee/ on·koy	hisp'ay p'iti/ unquy
wound	*k'ee*·ree	k'iri

HEALTH

WOMEN'S HEALTH

Could I see a female healer?
pahkh·tah *warh*·mee
hahm·*pekh*·wahn
hahm·pee·chee·*kui*·mahn?

I'm pregnant.
week·sah·*yokh*·mee *kah*·nee

I think I'm pregnant.
week·sah·*yoos*·choos
hee·nah kah·*shah*·nee

I haven't had my period
for ... weeks.
...·nyah yah·*wahr*·nee *mah*·nah
hah·*moon*·choo

WARMIKUNAQ QHALI KAYNIN

¿Paqta warmi
hampiqwan
hampichikuyman?

Wiksayuqmi kani.

Wiksayuschus
hina kashani.

...·ña yawarniy mana
hamunchu.

SPECIAL HEALTH NEEDS

I have ...   ...·*wahm*·mee kah·*shah*·nee
    anaemia   ah·nee·*mee*·yah
    asthma   *chah*·k'ee *oo*·hoo
    epilepsy   *wah*·nyui *on*·koy
    rheumatism   *too*·lyoo *nah*·nai

I suffer from allergies.
ah·leer·*hee*·koon *kah*·nee

I have a weak heart.
mah·nahn ah·*lyeen*·choo *son*·koy

I can't see very well.
mah·nahn ah·*lyeen*·tah
ree·*kui*·tah ah·tee·*nee*·choo

UNQUQKUNA QHALI KANANPAQ

...·wanmi kashani.
    animiya
    chak'i uhu
    wañuy unquy
    tullu nanay

Alirhikun kani.

Manan allinchu sunquy.

Manan allinta
rikuyta atinichu.

PARTS OF THE BODY   AYCHA KURKU KUNU

My ... hurts.
  ...ee/·nee nah·nah·*wah*·shahn

...-y/-niy nanawashan.

My ... is swollen.
  ...ee/·nee poon·*kees*·kah
  kah·shahn

...-y/-niy punkisqa
kashan.

I can't move my ...
  mah·nahn ...·*ee*·tah/·*nee*·tah
  koo·yoo·*chee*·tah
  ah·tee·*nee*·choo

Manan ...-yta/-niyta
kuyuchiyta
atinichu.

HEALTH

FIX IT

Remember, when using the -y/-niy or -yta/-niyta suffixes
with words, choose the -y or -yta ending when the root
word ends in a vowel, and the -niy or -niyta ending
when it ends in a consonant.

---

ankle	*chah*·kee mo·*k·ho*·choo	chaki muquchu
arm	*mah*·keel/*mahr*·k'ah	maki/marq'a
back	*wah*·sah	wasa
bladder	*hees*·p'ai *poo*·roo	hisp'ay puru
bone	*too*·lyoo	tullu
bottom	*see*·kee	siki
breast	*nyoo*·nyoo	ñuñu
buttock	*see*·kee *pah*·pahn	siki papan
cheek	*k'ahkh*·lyah	k'aklla
chest	*k·hahs*·ko	qhasqu
ear	*reen*·ree/*neen*·ree	rinri/ninri
elbow	k'oo·*koo*·choo/	k'ukuchu/
	koo·choos	kuchus
eye	*nyah*·wee	ñawi
face	*oo*·yah	uya
finger	roo·*k'ah*/*ree*·roo	ruk'a/riru
foot	*chah*·kee	chaki
forehead	*mah*·t'ee	mat'i

HEALTH

hand	*mah*·kee	*maki*
head	*oo*·mah	*uma*
heart	*son*·ko	*sunqu*
hip	*see*·kee *pah*·tah	*siki pata*
jaw/chin	*k'ah*·kee	*k'aki*
kidney	*roo*·roon;	*rurun;*
	wah·sah *roo*·roon	*wasa rurun*
knee	*mo*·ko/*kon*·kor	*muqu/qunqur*
leg	*chah*·kah	*chaka*
lips	*weer*·p'ah	*wirp'a*
liver	*koo*·*koo*·peen/	*kukupin/*
	k'eep·chahn	*k'ipchan*
lungs	*sor*·k'ahn	*surq'an*
mouth	*see*·mee	*simi*
nail	*see*·lyoo	*sillu*
neck	*koon*·kah	*kunka*
nose	*sen*·kah	*sinqa*
penis	*pee*·*chee*·koo/*pees*·ko	*pichiku/pisqu*
rib	*wahkh*·tah	*waqta*
shoulder	*reek*·rah	*rikra*
skin	*kah*·rah	*qara*
spine	*wah*·sah *too*·lyoo	*wasa tullu*
stomach	*week*·sah	*wiksa*
teeth	*kee*·roo	*kiru*
tongue	*kah*·lyoo	*qallu*
throat	*ton*·kor/*ton*·*ko*·ree/	*tunqur/tunquri/*
	k'ah·sah	*q'asa*
vagina	*rah*·k-hah	*rakha*
vein	*seer*·k'ah	*sirk'a*
waist	*we*·kow	*wiqaw*
wrist	*mah*·kee *mo*·ko	*maki muqu*

PACHAKUNAPAS RAYMIKUNAPAS
TIME, DATES & FESTIVALS

Time is flexibly defined in the Andes. While 'clock time' certainly exists, Andeans have set their schedules by the movement of the sun for centuries, and their ways of expressing the passing of time reflect this.

Despite the hard life of rural Andeans – or perhaps because of it – they find many reasons to celebrate. Weddings, baptisms, national and regional holidays, Carnival, Catholic holy days, patron saints' days and other traditional religious occasions are all reasons to take a break from work for a few hours or days.

TELLING THE TIME   URAMANTA RIMAY

Telling the time in Quechua is easy. To express the time in hours, you simply use the number for that hour, followed by *urasmi*, oo·*rahs*·mee:

It's (one) o'clock.
    (hokh) oo·*rahs*·mee   *(Huq) urasmi.*

To express the half hour, you add 'half', *kuskanniyuqmi*, koos·kahn·nee·*yokh*·mee, into the hour:

Half past one.
    hokh oo·rahs   *Huq uras kuskanniyuqmi.*
    koos·kahn·nee·*yokh*·mee

For any time between the hour and the half hour, you need to express how many minutes are added to the previous hour:

Quarter past one.
    hokh oo·rahs *choon*·kah   *Huq uras chunka*
    pees·*kah*·yokh   *pisqayuq*
    mee·noo·too·*yokh*·mee   *minutuyuqmi.*

What's the time?
ee·mah oo·rahs·mee kah·shahn?   ¿Ima urasmi kashan?

It's twenty past three.
keen·sah oo·rahs ees·kai   Kinsa uras iskay
choon·kah pees·kah·yokh   chunka pisqayuq
mee·noo·too·yokh·mee   minutuyuqmi.

Likewise, time between the half hour and the hour to come is expressed by how many minutes are lacking until the next full hour:

It's quarter to four.
choon·kah pees·kah·yokh   Chunka pisqayuq
mee·noo·too p·hahl·tahn   minutu phaltan
tah·wah oo·rahs·pahkh   tawa uraspaq.

DAYS OF THE WEEK   P'UNCHAYKUNA

Monday	loo·nees	lunis
Tuesday	mahr·tees	martis
Wednesday	meer·koo·lees	mirkulis
Thursday	hui·wees	huywis
Friday	weer·nees	wirnis
Saturday	sah·wah·roo	sawaru
Sunday	doo·meen·goo	dumingu

MONTHS   KILLAKUNA

January	ee·nee·roo kee·lyah	iniru killa
February	p·hyoo·ree·roo kee·lyah	phiwriru killa
March	mahr·soo kee·lyah	marsu killa
April	ow·reel kee·lyah	awril killa
May	mah·yoo kee·lyah	mayu killa
June	hoo·nee·yoo kee·lyah	huniyu killa
July	hoo·lee·yoo kee·lyah	huliyu killa
August	ah·woos·too kee·lyah	awustu killa

September	see·*teem*·ree *kee*·lyah	*sitimri killa*
October	ook·*too*·ree *kee*·lyah	*uktuwri killa*
November	noo·*weem*·bree *kee*·lyah	*nuwimbri killa*
December	dee·*seem*·ree *kee*·lyah	*disimri killa*

SEASONS

MIT'AKUNA

autumn	*po*·koy *mee*·t'ah	*puquy mit'a*
spring	*chee*·row *mee*·t'ah	*chiraw mit'a*
summer	*roo*·p-hai *mee*·t'ah	*ruphay mit'a*
winter	*chee*·ree *mee*·t'ah	*chiri mit'a*
dry season	*ch'ah*·kee *mee*·t'ah	*ch'aki mit'a*
rainy season	*pah*·rah *mee*·t'ah	*para mit'a*

TIME, DATES & FESTIVALS

BY THE SUN ...

In areas where people don't own watches, they tell the time by the sun's movements.

inti siqay;   *een*·tee *se*·kai;
inti lluqsimuy   *een*·tee lyokh·*see*·mui
  dawn/sunrise ('the sun comes up')

inti llipipimuy   *een*·tee lyee·pee·*pee*·mui
  sunrise ('flickering sun')

inti t'iksuy;   *een*·tee *t'eek*·sui;
qhata inti   k-*hah*·tah *een*·tee
  late afternoon ('the sun leans'/'sloping sun')

inti haykuy   *een*·tee *hai*·kui
  sunset (sundown/'the sun goes down behind
  the horizon')

intiq lluqsinan   *een*·tekh llokh·*see*·nahn
  east ('where the sun comes up')

intiq chinkanan   *een*·tekh cheen·*kah*·nahn
  west ('where the sun disappears')

TIME, DATES & FESTIVALS

DATES

PACHAKUNA

What's the date today?
  ee·mah pah·*chah*·tahkh *koo*·nahn?

¿Ima pachataq kunan?

It's 18 October.
  choon·kah poo·sahkh·*nee*·yokh
  ook·*too*·ree *kee*·lyahn

Chunka pusaqniyuq uktuwri killan.

Present

Kunan Pacha

now	*koo*·nahn	kunan
today	*koo*·nahn p'oon·chai	kunan p'unchay
tonight	ch'ee·*see*·mahn	ch'isiman
this ...	*koo*·nahn ...	kunan ...
morning	too·tah·*mahn*·tahn	tutamantan
afternoon	*een*·tee teek·*sui*·pee;	inti t'iksuypi;
	tai·*ree*·mahn	tayriman
night	*too*·tah	tuta
week	see·*mah*·nah	simana
month	*kee*·lyah	killa
year	*wah*·tah	wata

Past

Qayna Pacha

yesterday	*kai*·nah p'oon·chai	qayna p'unchay
day before	kai·*neem*·pah	qaynimpa
yesterday	p'oon·chai	p'unchay
yesterday ...	*kai*·nah ...	qayna ...
morning	too·tah·*mahn*·tahn	tutamantan
afternoon	*een*·tee	inti
evening	t'eek·*sui*·pee/*ch'ee*·see	t'iksuypi/ch'isi
last ...	*kai*·nah ...	qayna ...
night	*too*·tah	tuta
week	see·*mah*·nah	simana
month	*kee*·lyah	killa
year	*wah*·tah	wata
since (May)	(mah·yoo kee·lyah)·*mahn*·tah	(mayu killa)·manta

Future

		Hawa Pacha
tomorrow ...	pah·*kah*·reen ...	*paqarin ...*
morning	too·tah·*mahn*·tahn	*tutamantan*
afternoon	*een*·tee teek·*sui*·pee;	*inti t'iksuypi;*
	tai·*ree*·mahn	*tayriman*
evening	*ch'ee*·see	*ch'isi*
day after	*meen*·ch·hah	*minchha*
tomorrow		
next ...	*k'ah*·yah/*hah*·wah ...	*q'aya/hawa ...*
week	see·*mah*·nah	*simana*
month	*kee*·lyah	*killa*
year	*wah*·tah	*wata*

in (five) minutes
    (pees·kah) mee·noo·too·*mahn*·tah   *(pisqa) minutumanta*

until (June)
    (hoo·*nee*·yoo kee·lyah)·*kah*·mah   *(huniyu killa)-kama*

DURING THE DAY

		P'UNCHAYPI
afternoon	*een*·tee *t'eek*·sui; *tai*·ree	*inti t'iksuy; tayri*
dawn	*een*·tee *se*·kai/	*inti siqay/*
	lyokh·see	*lluqsiy*
day	*p'oon*·chai/*p'oon*·chow	*p'unchay/p'unchaw*
early	too·tah·lyah·*mahn*·tah	*tutallamanta*
evening	*ch'ee*·seen	*ch'isin*
lunchtime	*mee*·k·hui *oo*·rah	*mikhuy ura*
midday	*chow*·pee *p'oon*·chai	*chawpi p'unchay*
midnight	*chow*·pee *too*·tah	*chawpi tuta*
morning	too·tah·*mahn*·tahn	*tutamantan*
night	*too*·tah	*tuta*
noon	*chow*·pee *p'oon*·chai	*chawpi p'unchay*

TIME, DATES & FESTIVALS

TIMES, DATES & FESTIVALS

FESTIVALS & NATIONAL HOLIDAYS

RAYMIKUNAPAS HATUN P'UNCHAYKUNAPAS

The Andean countries are predominantly Catholic, and numerous holy days and ancient traditions fill the celebration calendar. Any religious event is also a social event, a reason to gather and celebrate.

Inti Raymi   *een·tee rai·mee*

The 'Festival of the Sun' honours the sun god, the highest of the Andean deities, and is a week-long celebration held during the winter solstice. The high point of the festival occurs in Sacsayhuamán, just outside of Cuzco. 24 June is the day of *Inti Raymi*, which marks the beginning of the sun's New Year. It was banned for centuries by the Catholic church, but continued to be held in secret.

Mamacha Kandilarya   mah·*mah*·chah
                                        kahn·dee·*lahr*·yah

The Festival of the Virgin of the Candelaria. She is the patron saint of both Bolivia and Peru and is known throughout South America as a worker of great miracles. Festivities in her honour – parades, music, dancing, food and drink, and an interesting mix of Andean and Catholic religious rituals – begin a week prior to 2 February. The colour and incomparable majesty of these events is a prelude to Carnival.

Karnawal   kahr·*nah*·wahl

Carnival is celebrated throughout South America, but takes on a uniquely Andean flavour in Bolivia, Peru and Ecuador, where each region has its own special traditions. The week-long celebrations take place the week before Ash Wednesday on the Catholic calendar. Everyone lives it up before the fasting and sacrifice of Lent.

Día de Todos los Santos   *dee*·ah de *to*·dos los *sahn*·tos
Día de los Muertos   *dee*·ah de los *mwer*·tos

All Saints' Day on 1 November and All Souls' Day, the next day, are more than a simple observance honouring the saints and departed family members – they have become enmeshed with Andean beliefs and practices for honouring the dead. After attending Mass, community members prepare a feast, often served in the local cemetery so that departed family members can participate. There are always some favourite dishes – often lavishly decorated – of those who have passed away.

Nawida P'unchay   nah·*wee*·dah *p'oon*·chai

Midnight Mass and street celebrations with music, dancing, food and drinks on Christmas Eve and Christmas Day are common. You'll see the nativity scene everywhere in homes and churches. In less Christian areas, Christmas may be celebrated as a harvest festival.

Año Nuevo   *ah·*nyo *nwe·*vo

New Year's Eve and New Year's Day are included in the general Christmas festivities. Regional traditions involve processions, gatherings and public dancing where everyone joins in. In some parts of Bolivia, the Christmas season celebrations last until the end of January.

Día de los Reyes Magos   *dee·*ah de los *re·*yes *mah·*gos

Epiphany, or the Feast of the Three Kings, on 6 January, marks the end of the Christmas season. It's the day children traditionally receive their Christmas gifts.

Fiestas Patrias   *fyes·*tahs *pah·*tryahs

Every Latin American country celebrates the day it achieved independence from Spain. It's a time of parties and demonstrations of patriotism, people wave flags and sing national anthems during the colourful parades. Peru's Independence Day is 28 July, Bolivia's 6 August and Ecuador's 10 August.

Día del Santo Patrón   *dee·*ah del *sahn·*to pah·*tron*

National, regional and local patron saints' days vary according to the saint being honoured. The festivities may be one to several days in length, and generally include music and dancing, as well as special Masses and services. They are as much a social event and party as a dedicated religious observance – saints' day celebrations are a treat not to be missed.

Aniversario de Fundación   ah·nee·ver·*sah·*ryo de foon·dah·*syon*

Many cities, towns and villages celebrate the anniversary of their founding. Since these are secular celebrations, there may or may not be a special Mass offered, but there'll always be typical Andean festivities.

CHRISTENINGS & WEDDINGS

ULIYAYKUNAPAS KASARAKUYKUNAPAS

Given the wide variety of traditions, weddings can be performed and celebrated in very different ways. Christenings, on the other hand, are fairly uniform due to the influence of Catholicism. They're an all-day affair, accompanied by a feast put on by the godparents. As with other celebrations, there is much singing and dancing, eating and drinking.

Congratulations!
  koo·see·*koos*·pah
  kow·sah·koon·*kee*·chees!
           ¡Kusikuspa
           kawsakunkichis!

To the bride and groom!
  kah·sah·rahkh·*koo*·nah
  how·*kah*·lyah kow·sah·*choon*·koo!
           ¡Kasaraqkuna
           hawkalla kawsachunku!

baptism	oo·lee·yoo/wow·*tee*·soo	uliyu/wawtisu
to baptise/ christen	oo·lee·yai/oo·*noo*·chai/ wow·*tee*·sai	uliyay/unuchay/ wawtisay
to celebrate	k'o·choo·*ree*·chee/ fees·*tee*·hai	q'uchurichiy/ phistihay
to celebrate (a birthday)	fees·*tah*·kui	phistakuy
festival	*rai*·mee	raymi
gift	ree·koo·*chee*·kui	rikuchikuy
goddaughter	ai·*hah*·rah	ayhara
godfather	pah·*ree*·noo	parinu
godmother	mah·*ree*·nah	marina
godparent	mahr·*k'ah*·ke	marq'aqi
godson	ai·*hah*·roo	ayharu
holiday	*hah*·toon fees·tah	hatun phista
party	fees·*tah*	phista
wedding	kahk·sah·*rah*·kui	kasarakuy
wedding present	kah·sah·rahkh·koo·*nah*·pahkh ree·koo·*chee*·kui	kasaraqkunapaq rikuchikuy

TIME, DATES & FESTIVALS

TOASTS & CONDOLENCES	**ANQUSAYKUNAPAS LLAKIPAYKUNAPAS**

Bon appetit!
  mees·k'ee·lyah·*tah*·nyah
  mee·*k-hoo*·kui!
  ¡Misk'illataña mikhukuy!

Bon voyage!
  ah·lyeen·*lyah*·nyah poo·*ree*·kui!
  ¡Allinllaña purikuy!

Cheers!
  ook·yai·*koo*·soon!
  ¡Ukyaykusun!

Good luck!
  ah·lyeen sah·*mee*·yokh kai!
  ¡Allin samiyuq kay!

Hope it goes well!
  ee·*chah*·pahs roo·wahs·*kai*·kee
  ah·lyeen *kahn*·mahn!
  ¡Ichapas ruwasqayki allin kanman!

What bad luck!
  ee·mah k-*hen*·chah!
  ¡Ima qhincha!

Never mind!
  mah·nah ee·mah·nahn·*pahs*·choo!
  ¡Mana imananpaschu!

Get well soon!
  oos·*k-hai*·lyah ah·lyeen·*yah*·yai!
  ¡Usqhaylla allinyayay!

I'm very sorry.
  ahn·*chah*·tahn lyah·kee·*pai*·kee
  Anchatan llakipayki.

My deepest sympathy.
  seen·*chee*·tahn lyah·kee·*pai*·kee
  Sinchitan llakipayki.

The numbers from zero to 10 each have their own name. These 'basic' numbers are also used to form the numbers from 11 to 19, which are expressed as '10 with one' through to '10 with nine'. The suffix *-yuq, -yokh* 'with', is added to the end of units, not to the tens. Forming the tens is easy too: 20 is 'two tens', 30 is 'three tens', and so on. Remember that when a number ends in a consonant, the suffix *-ni* needs to be added before the suffix *-yuq*. For example, the number 11 is formed by joining *huq* for 'one' and *chunka* for '10' – *chunka huqniyuq, choon·kah hokh·nee·yokh*.

To count from 100 onwards, you use the same system as for the numbers one to 100. Thus the number 2002 would be *iskay waranqa iskayniyuq, ees·kai wah·rahn·kah ees·kai·nee·yokh* (lit: two thousand two-with).

CARDINAL NUMBERS   IMAKAQ YUPAKUNA

0	*ch'oo·*sahkh	*ch'usaq*
1	hokh	*huq*
2	*ees·*kai	*iskay*
3	*keen·*sah	*kinsa*
4	*tah·*wah	*tawa*
5	*pees·*kah	*pisqa*
6	*sokh·*tah	*suqta*
7	*kahn·*chees	*qanchis*
8	*poo·*sakh	*pusaq*
9	*ees·*kon	*isqun*
10	*choon·*kah	*chunka*
11	*choon·*kah hokh·*nee·*yokh	*chunka huqniyuq*
12	*choon·*kah ees·kai·*nee·*yokh	*chunka iskayniyuq*

13	*choon*·kah keen·*sah*·yokh	*chunka kinsayuq*
14	*choon*·kah tah·*wah*·yokh	*chunka tawayuq*
15	*choon*·kah pees·*kah*·yokh	*chunka pisqayuq*
16	*choon*·kah sokh·*tah*·yokh	*chunka suqtayuq*
17	*choon*·kah	*chunka*
	kahn·chees·*nee*·yokh	*qanchisniyuq*
18	*choon*·kah	*chunka*
	poo·sahkh·*nee*·yokh	*pusaqniyuq*
19	*choon*·kah	*chunka*
	ees·kon·*nee*·yokh	*isqunniyuq*
20	*ees*·kay *choon*·kah	*iskay chunka*
21	*ees*·kay *choon*·kah	*iskay chunka*
	hokh·*nee*·yokh	*huqniyuq*
22	*ees*·kay *choon*·kah	*iskay chunka*
	ees·kai·*nee*·yokh	*iskayniyuq*
30	keen·*sah choon*·kah	*kinsa chunka*
40	*tah*·wah *choon*·kah	*tawa chunka*
50	pees·kah *choon*·kah	*pisqa chunka*
60	sokh·tah *choon*·kah	*suqta chunka*
70	*kahn*·chees *choon*·kah	*qanchis chunka*
80	poo·sakh *choon*·kah	*pusaq chunka*
90	*ees*·kon *choon*·kah	*isqun chunka*
100	*pah*·chahkh	*pachak*
1000	wah·*rahn*·kah	*waranqa*
1,000,000	*hoo*·noo	*hunu*

ORDINAL NUMBERS   ÑIQI YUPAKUNA

To form ordinal numbers, add either *ñiqin, nye*·ken, meaning 'order' or *kaq,* kahkh, meaning 'that which is' to the cardinal number; these endings can be used interchangeably. Note that '1st' is an exception:

1st	*nyow*·pahkh kahkh	*ñawpaq kaq*
2nd	*ees*·kai kahkh	*iskay kaq*
3rd	keen·*sah* kahkh	*kinsa kaq*

FRACTIONS

1/2	*ees*·kai *tah*·k'ah	*iskay taq'a*
1/3	*keen*·sah *tah*·k'ah	*kinsa taq'a*
1/4	*tah*·wah *tah*·k'ah	*tawa taq'a*
3/4	*keen*·sah *tah*·wah *tah*·k'ah	*kinsa tawa taq'a*

P'AKIKUNA

AMOUNTS

HAYK'AKAKUNA

How many/much?	*hai*·k'ah?	¿*Hayk'a?*
I need ...	...tah moo·*mah*·nee	*...-ta munani.*
all	*lyah*·pahn/*too*·kui/lyoo	*llapan/tukuy/lliw*
(just) a little	*ahs*·lyah/*pee*·see/ chee·*kah*·lyah	*aslla/pisi/ chikalla*
some/a few	wah·*kee*·lyahn/ *pee*·see/*ahs*·lyah	*wakillan/ pisi/aslla*
enough	chai·*lyah*	*chaylla*
few	*ahs*·lyah; ahs pee·*see*·lyah; *chee*·kahn; *toom*·pah	*aslla; as pisilla; chikan; tumpa*
less	*pee*·see	*pisi*
many/much/ a lot	*ahs*·k-hah; *yoo*·pah; mai *chee*·kahn; mai·*too*·kui	*askha; yupa; may chikan; maytukuy*
more	ahs·*tah*·wahn	*astawan*
none/nothing	*mah*·nah ee·*mah*·pahs	*mana imapas*
once	hokh *koot*·ee	*huq kuti*
plenty	*lyah*·sahkh	*llasaq*
some	*toom*·pah/*ahs*·lyah	*tumpa/aslla*
too many/much	*ahs*·k-hah/*seen*·chee/ mai·*too*·kui/*lyah*·sahkh	*askha/sinchi/ maytukuy/llasaq*

JUST GIVE ME ...

a bottle	hokh woo·*tee*·lyah	*huq wutilla*
a dozen	*choon*·kah	*chunka*
	ees·kai·nee·yokh·neen·teen;	*iskayniyuq-nintin;*
	hokh doo·*see*·nah	*huq dusina*
half a kilo	*meed*·yoo kee·loo	*midyu kilu*
half a dozen	*meed*·yah doo·*see*·nah	*midya dusina*
a kilo	wah·*rahn*·kah *ahkh*·noo	*waranqa-aqnu*
a hand full	*hahp*-h·t'ai	*hapht'ay*
two handfuls	*pot*·koi	*putquy*
100 grams	*pah*·chahkh-*ahkh*·noo	*pachak-aqnu*
a packet	hokh pah·*kee*·tee	*huq pakiti*
a pair	ees·kai·*neen*·teen	*iskaynintin*
a piece	*ahkh*·noo	*aqnu*
a pile	*ko*·too/*row*·k-hah/*moon*·toon/*tow*·kah	*qutu/rawkha/muntun/tawqa*

USQHAYLLAPAQÑA
EMERGENCIES

In rural and remote areas, Quechua could be vital.

Fire!	*nee*·nah roo·*p·hah*·shahn!	¡Nina ruphashan!
Go away!	*ree*·pui!;	¡Ripuy!;
	lyokh·see kai·*mahn*·tah!	¡Lluqsiy kaymanta!
Help!	yah·nah·*pah*·wai!	¡Yanapaway!
Stop!	*sah*·yai!	¡Sayay!
Thief!	*soo*·wah!	¡Suwa!
Watch out!	pahkh·*tah*·tahkh!/	¡Paqtataq!/
	ah·chah·*chow*!	¡Achacháw!

It's an emergency.
   seen·chee os·k·hai·*pahkh*·mee;
   nee·shoo pree·see·*sahkh*·mee

Sinchi usqhaypaqmi;
Nishu prisisaqmi.

Could you help us please?
   ah·*lyee*·choo yah·nah·pah·
   wahn·kee·koo·*mahn*·choo?

¿Allichu yanapa-
wankikumanchu?

Could I please use the telephone?
   ah·*lyee*·choo tee·lee·foo·*noo*·wahn
   ree·mai·kui·*mahn*·choo?

¿Allichu tiliphunuwan
rimaykuymanchu?

I'm lost.
   cheen·*kahs*·kahn kah·*shah*·nee;
   cheen·*kahs*·kahn poo·ree·*shah*·nee

Chinkasqan kashani;
Chinkasqan purishani.

Where are the toilets?
   mai·*pee*·tahkh hees·p'ah·*koo*·nah
   kah·shahn?; mai·*pee*·tahkh
   hees·p'ah·*kui*·mahn?

¿Maypitaq hisp'akuna
kashan?; ¿Maypitaq
hisp'akuyman?

Call a doctor/healer!
   mee·dee·*koo*·tah/hahm·*pekh*·tah
   wahkh·*yah*·mui!

¡Midikuta/Hampiqta
waqyamuy!

I'm ill.
   on·*kos*·kahn kah·*shah*·nee

Unqusqan kashani.

My friend is ill.
   rekh·see·nah·kokh·mah·*see*·mee
   on·*ko*·shahn

Riqsinakuqmasiymi
unqushan.

POLICE

WARDIYA

Call the police!

wahr·dee·*yah*·tah wahkh·*yah*·mui!   ¡Wardiyata waqyamuy!

Where's the police station?

mai·*pee*·tahkh koo·mee·sah·*ree*·yah   ¿Maypitaq kumisariya
kah·shahn?   kashan?

I've been robbed.

soo·wah·chee·koo·*roo*·neen   Suwachikurqunin.

My ... was/	...·*ee*·tahn soo·wah	...-ytan suwa
were stolen.	ah·*pah*·koon	apakun.
I've lost	...·*ee*·tahn	...-ytan
my ...	cheen·kah·chee·*roo*·nee	chinkachirquni.
backpack	ke·pee	qipi
bags	mah·lee·tai·koo·*nah*·tahn	malitaykunatan
handbag	wah·*yah*·kah/ch'oos·pah	wayaqa/ch'uspa
money	*kol*·ke	qulqi
papers	doo·koo·meen·tui·	dukumintuy-
	koo·*nah*·tahn	kunatan
wallet	*kol*·ke choo·*rah*·nah/	qulqi churana/
	wee·lyee·*tee*·rah	willitira
(not) guilty	(*mah*·nah) hoo·*chah*·yokh	(mana) huchayuq
police officer	*tai*·tah wahr·*dee*·yah	tayta wardiya
police station	koo·mee·sah·*ree*·yah	kumisariya
rape	ahl·*ko*·chai	alquchay
robbery/theft	soo·*wah*·kui	suwakuy

ENGLISH – QUECHUA DICTIONARY

A

English	Pronunciation	Quechua
to be able	ah·tee	atiy
above	hah·wahn·pee	hawanpi
abroad	kah·roo lyahkh·tah	karu llaqta
to accept	ui·nee	uyniy
accident	ahkh·see·deen·tee	aksidinti
accommodation	kor·pah·chah·nah	qurpachana
ache	nah·nai	nanay
across (from)	cheem·pah·pee	chimpapi
adult	wee·nyai hoon·t'ahs·kah • kaly·pah·yokh	wiñay hunt'asqa • kallpayuq
advice	yoo·yai koy	yuyay quy
to advise (inform)	wee·lyai	willay
to advise (counsel)	yoo·yai·chai	yuyaychay
aeroplane	ah·wee·yoon	awiyun
to be afraid	mahn·chah·kui	manchakuy
afterwards	chai·mahn·tah·kah	chaymantaqa
again	hokh·mahn·tah	huqmanta
against	koon·trah	kuntra
ago (a while ago)	hokh rah·too·nyah	huq ratuña
to agree to	oo·yah·kui	uyakuy
ahead	nyow·pahkh	ñawpaq
air	wai·rah	wayra
alcohol	wahkh·too	waqtu
all	lyah·pah	llapa
to allow	sah·ke·lyai	saqillay
almost	yah·kah	yaqa
alone	sah·pah	sapa
already	·nyah	-ña
also (interchangeable)	·pees • ·pahs	-pis • -pas
although	chai·pahs	chaypas
always	pah·sahkh koo·tee·lyah	pasaq kutilla
among	oo·k·hoo·pee	ukhupi
ancient	nyow·pah	ñawpa
angry	p·hee·nyah	phiña
another	hokh	huq
to answer	koo·tee·chee	kutichiy
anything	ee·mah·lyah·pahs	imallapas
to argue	choo·rah·nah·kui	churanakuy
to arrive	chai·yai	chayay
to ask (a question)	tah·pui	tapuy
to ask (for something)	mah·nyah·kui	mañakuy
awful	mah·p'ah	map'a

B

baby (human)	*wah·*wah	wawa
baby (animal)	*oo·*nyah	uña
babysitter	*wah·*wah k-*hah·*wahkh	wawa qhawaq
backpack	*k'ee·*pee	q'ipi
bad	*mah·*nah *ah·*lyeen	mana allin
bag (large)	wah·*yah·*kah	wayaqa
bag (small)	*ch'oos·*pah	ch'uspa
baggage	mah·*lee·*tah	malita
ball	pee·*loo·*tah	piluta
band (music)	koo·*see·*tui	kusituy
bank (shore)	*kahn·*too	kantu
baptism	oo·*lee·*yai	uliyay
to barter	ch-*hah·*lai	chhalay
basket	kah·*nahs·*tah	kanasta
to bathe	ahr·*mah·*kui	armakuy
bathroom	*bah·*nyoo	bañu
to be	kai	kay
to bear (put up with)	ah·*tee·*pai	atipay
bear (animal)	oo·*koo·*koo	ukuku
beautiful	*soo·*mahkh	sumaq
bed	poo·*nyoo·*nah	puñuna
bedroom	poo·*nyoo·*nah *kwahr·*too	puñuna kwartu
before (time)	nyow·*pahkh·*tah	ñawpaqta
to begin	kah·*lyah·*ree	qallariy
behind	k-*he·*pah	qhipa
to believe (religious)	*ee·*nee • *ee·*nyee	iniy • iñiy
below	oo·*rai	uray
beside	wahkh·*tahn·*pee	waqtanpi
besides (furthermore)	hee·*nahs·*pah	hinaspa
better	*ahs·*wahn *ah·*lyeen	aswan allin
bicycle	wee·see·kee·*lee·*tah	wisiklita
big	*hah·*toon	hatun
bigger	*ahs·*wahn *hah·*toon	aswan hatun
birthday	*wah·*tah hoon·*t'ai	wata hunt'ay
to bite (any creature)	kah·*nee	kaniy
to bite (of an insect)	*k'oo·*tui	k'utuy
to bite (of a dog; chew off something)	k-*hah·*chui	khachuy
blanket	kah·*tah • *choo·*see	qata • chusi
to bleed	yah·*wahr·*chai	yawarchay
blind (adj)	nyow·*sah	ñawsa
blood	yah·*wahr	yawar
to bloom/blossom	*see·*sai	sisay
blue (of eyes only)	k-*ho·*see	qhusi

boat	*wahm·poo*	*wampu*
body	*ai·chah koor·koo*	*aycha kurku*
book	*lyoo·roo*	*liwru*
border	*sai·wah*	*saywa*
bored/boring	*ah·mees·kah*	*amisqa*
to borrow	*mah·nui·pee mah·nyai*	*manuypi mañay*
both	*ees·kai·neen*	*iskaynin*
to bother	*ch'ekh·mee*	*ch'iqmiy*
bottle	*woo·tee·lyah*	*wutilla*
bottle opener	*woo·tee·lyah kee·chah·nah*	*wutilla kichana*
bottom (body)	*see·kee*	*siki*
boy	*er·ke*	*irqi*
boyfriend	*yah·nah*	*yana*
bread	*t'ahn·tah*	*t'anta*
to break	*p'ah·kee*	*p'akiy*
breakfast	*too·tah·mahn·tah mee·k·hoo·nah*	*tutamanta mikhuna*
breasts	*nyoo·nyoo*	*ñuñu*
to breathe	*sah·mah·ree*	*samariy*
bridge	*chah·kah*	*chaka*
to bring	*ah·pah·mui*	*apamuy*
broken	*p'ah·kees·kah*	*p'akisqa*
to build	*per·kah·chai*	*pirqachay*
building	*hah·toon wah·see*	*hatun wasi*
bull	*too·roo*	*turu*
bullfighting	*too·roo pookh·lyai*	*turu pukllay*
burn	*roo·p-hai*	*ruphay*
to burn	*roo·p-hah·chee*	*ruphachiy*
busy (employed)	*roo·wah·nah·yokh*	*ruwanayuq*
busy (no free time)	*mah·nah kah·sekh*	*mana qasiq*
but	*ee·chah·kah*	*ichaqa*
butter	*mahn·tee·kee·lyah*	*mantikilla*
to buy	*rahn·tee*	*rantiy*

C

cabbage	*koo·lees*	*kulis*
calf	*oo·nyah*	*uña*
to call (by shouting)	*wahkh·yai*	*waqyay*
to call (to name)	*soo·tee·chai*	*sutichay*
can (to be able)	*ah·tee*	*atiy*
can (of food)	*lah·tah*	*lata*
can opener	*lah·tah kee·chah·nah*	*lata kichana*
candles	*bee·lah·koo·nah*	*bilakuna*
capital city	*oo·mah lyahkh·tah*	*uma llaqta*

car	kah·rroo	karru
care	k-hah·wai	qhaway
to carry (on the back)	k'e·pee	q'ipiy
cassette	kah·see·tee	kasiti
Catholic	kah·too·lee·koo	katuliku
cave	mah·ch'ai	mach'ay
to celebrate	k'oo·choo·kui	q'uchukuy
cemetery	ah·yah p'ahm·pah·nah	aya p'ampana
ceramic	k'akhk·rah	k'akra
chair	tee·yah·nah	tiyana
to change (become different)	hokh·nee·rah·yai	huqnirayay
to change (exchange)	kahm·bee·yai	kambiyay
to cheat	k'o·tui	q'utuy
cheese	kee·soo	kisu
chest	k-hahs·ko	qhasqu
chewing gum	cheek·lee	chikli
chicha (maize beer)	ah·hah • ah·k-hah	aha • aqha
chicha bar	ah·hah·wah·see	ahawasi
chicken	wahly·pah	wallpa
child	wah·wah	wawa
chocolate	mees·k'ee • choo·koo·lah·tee	misk'i • chukulati
to choose	ahkh·lyai	akllay
church	een·lee·sah	inlisa
cigarette	see·yah·roo	siyaru
cinema	see·nee	sini
city	lyahkh·tah	llaqta
clean (of objects)	lui·loo	luylu
clean (of water)	ch'oo·yah	ch'uya
to clean	pee·chai	pichay
cliff	kah·kah	qaqa
to climb	wee·chai	wichay
clock	ree·lookh	riluh
to close	wees·k'ai	wisq'ay
close (near)	sees·pah	sispa
clothes	p'ah·chah	p'acha
coat	sah·koo	saku
coast	koos·tah	kusta
to collect	pah·lyai	pallay
colour	lyeem·pee	llimpi
to come	hah·mui	hamuy
comedian	ah·see·chee·kokh	asichikuq
to comfort	kahly·pah·chah·ree	kallpachariy
to communicate	wee·lyai	willay
community	ai·lyoo	ayllu

ENGLISH – QUECHUA DICTIONARY

English	Pronunciation	Quechua
community leader	hah·*mow*·t'ah	*hamawt'a*
constipation	k'ees·kee	*k'iski*
to cook	wai·k'ui	*wayk'uy*
corn	sah·rah	*sara*
corn on the cob	chokh·lyo	*chuqllu*
corner (outside)	k'oo·choo	*k'uchu*
corner (inside)	hoo·k'ee	*huk'i*
to cost	kwees·tai	*kwistay*
country (nation)	lyahkh·tah	*llaqta*
countryside	pahm·pah	*pampa*
cough	ch'oo·hoo • oo·hoo	*ch'uhu • uhu*
to cough	oo·hui	*uhuy*
to count	yoo·pai	*yupay*
courtyard	kahn·chah	*kancha*
cow	wah·kah	*waka*
crazy	wah·k'ah	*waq'a*
to cross	cheem·pai	*chimpay*
cross (angry)	p-hee·*nyahs*·kah	*phiñasqa*
crowd	tahn·tah	*tanta*
to cry	wah·kai	*waqay*
cup	sui·k'oo	*suyk'u*
cup (Incas ceremonial)	ke·roo	*qiru*
to cure	hahm·pee	*hampiy*
to cut	koo·chui	*kuchuy*

D

English	Pronunciation	Quechua
daily	sah·pah p'oon·chai	*sapa p'unchay*
damp	ho·k'o	*huq'u*
dance	too·sui	*tusuy*
to dance	too·sui	*tusuy*
danger	mahn·chai	*manchay*
dark (night)	too·tah	*tuta*
to get dark	too·tah·yai	*tutayay*
date of birth	wah·tah hoon·t'ai	*wata hunt'ay*
dawn	ee·lyah·ree • rahn·k-hee	*illariy • rankhi*
day	p'oon·chai	*p'unchay*
dead	wah·nyoos·kah	*wañusqa*
deaf	oo·pah	*upa*
to decide	kah·mah·ree·kui	*kamarikuy*
deep	oo·k-hoo	*ukhu*
delay	oo·nai	*unay*
to delay	oo·nai	*unay*
delicious	mees·k'ee	*misk'i*
dentist	kee·roo see·k'ekh	*kiru sik'iq*
to deny	mah·nahn nee	*manan niy*

to depart	lyokh·see	lluqsiy
descendent	k-he·pah wee·nyai	qhipa wiñay
desert	ah·ko pahm·pah	aqu pampa
to detour	wahkh·lyee	waqlliy
diarrhoea	k'e·chah	q'icha
to have diarrhoea	k'e·chai	q'ichay
to die	wah·nyui	wañuy
different	hokh·nee·rahkh	huqniraq
difficult	sah·sah	sasa
to direct	yah·chah·chee	yachachiy
dirty	k-hahr·kah	kharka
to disturb	tah·koo·ree	takuriy
dizzy	oo·mah moo·yoos·kah	uma muyusqa
to do/make	roo·wai	ruway
doctor	dookh·toor	duktur
done	roo·wahs·kah	ruwasqa
door	poon·koo	punku
to draw	se·k'en·chai	siq'inchay
dream/to dream	mos·k-hoy	musqhuy
dress	p'ah·chah	p'acha
to dress (oneself)	p'ah·chah·lyee·kui	p'achallikuy
to dress (someone else)	p'ah·chah·lyee·chee	p'achallichiy
drink/to drink	ookh·yai	ukyay
drug	hahm·pee	hampi
drugstore	hahm·pee·yokh wah·see	hampiyuq wasi
drum (small)	teen·yah	tinya
drum (large)	wahn·kahr	wankar
drunk	mah·chahkh	machaq
to get drunk	mah·chai	machay
dry	ch'ah·kee	ch'aki

E

each	sah·pah	sapa
early morning	too·tah·lyah·mahn·tah	tutallamanta
early afternoon	ah·lyeen·pee·rahkh	allinpiraq
to earn (money)	tah·ree	tariy
earth (soil)	aly·pah	allpa
the Earth	kay pah·chah	kay pacha
earth goddess (Mother Earth)	pah·chah·mah·mah	Pachamama
earthquake	pah·chah koo·yui	pacha kuyuy
east	een·tee lyokh·see·mui	inti lluqsimuy
easy	fah·seel	phasil

ENGLISH – QUECHUA DICTIONARY

English	Pronunciation	Quechua
to eat	*mee*·k-hui	mikhuy
to educate	yah·*chah*·chee	yachachiy
education	yah·chai	yachay
eggs	roon·too	runtu
to elect	ahk·lyai	akllay
electric light	loos	lus
to embarrass	p'en·*kah*·kui	p'inqakuy
embarrassed	p'en·*kahs*·kah	p'inqasqa
empire	tah·wahn·teen·*soo*·yoo	tawantinsuyu
empty	ch'oo·sahkh	ch'usaq
end	too·kui	tukuy
English	een·lees	inlis
to enjoy oneself	oo·sah·*chee*·kui	usachikuy
enough	chai·*lyah*·nyah	chayllaña
to enter	hai·kui	haykuy
to entertain	k'o·too·*ree*·chee	q'uturichiy
every	lyoo	lliw
everyone	lyoo·*neen*·koo	lliwninku
everything	*lyah*·pah	llapa
everywhere	mai·*pee*·pahs	maypipas
exact(ly)	k'ah·pahkh	k'apak
to exchange (products)	ch-hah·lai	chhalay
to exhibit	ree·koo·*ree*·chee	rikurichiy
to exist	kai	kay
to expect	soo·yai	suyay
expensive	ahn·chah chah·*nee*·yokh	ancha chaniyuq
to explain	yah·*chah*·chee	yachachiy

F

English	Pronunciation	Quechua
to fall	oor·mai	urmay
family	fah·*mee*·lyah	phamilla
famous	rekh·*sees*·kah	riqsisqa
far	kah·roo	karu
farm	chahkh·rah	chakra
farmer	*chahkh*·rah roo·nah	chakra runa
farmyard	kahn·chah	kancha
fast (movement)	p-hah·*wai*·lyah	phawaylla
fast (passage of time)	rah·*too*·lyah	ratulla
fat (grease)	wee·rah	wira
fault	hoo·chah	hucha
fava beans	hah·wahs	hawas
fear	mahn·*chah*·kui	manchakuy
to feed	kah·rai	qaray

to feel (sentiments)	*lyahkh·lyai*	*llakllay*
to feel (touch)	*lyah·mee*	*llamiy*
fence	*ken·chah*	*qincha*
festival	*rai·mee*	*raymi*
to fetch	*poo·sah·mui*	*pusamuy*
fever	*roo·*p-hah	*rupha*
few	*pee·see*	*pisi*
fiancé/fiancée	*oor·pee*	*urpi*
field (cultivated)	*chahkh·rah*	*chakra*
fight/to fight	ow·kah·*nah*·kui	*awqanakuy*
to fill	*hoon·*t'ai	*hunt'ay*
to find (something lost)	*tah·ree*	*tariy*
to finish	*too·kui*	*tukuy*
fire	*nee·nah*	*nina*
first	*nyow·*pahkh	*ñawpaq*
flashlight	k'ahn·*chah*·nah	*k'anchana*
flat (adj)	*p'ahl·*tah	*p'alta*
flat place	*pahm·pah*	*pampa*
flea	*pee·kee*	*piki*
flower	*t'ee·kah*	*t'ika*
flour	*hah·*k'oo	*hak'u*
to fly	p-hah·wai	*phaway*
fog	*pah·*chah p-hoo·yoo	*pacha phuyu*
to follow	*kah·tee*	*qatiy*
food	mee·*k·hoo*·nah	*mikhuna*
foreigner	*hah·*wah roo·nah	*hawa runa*
forest	*mahly·kee mahly·kee*	*mallki mallki*
forever	wee·nyai·*pah·chah*	*wiñaypacha*
to forget	*kon·kai*	*qunqay*
to forgive	pahm*·pah·chai*	*pampachay*
fort/fortress	poo·*kah·rah*	*pukara*
fortune teller	*wah·*tokh	*watuq*
free (at liberty)	*kes·pee*	*qispi*
free (no cost)	*yahn·kahn*	*yanqan*
to freeze	*kah·*sai	*qasay*
friend	rekh·see·nah·kokh·*mah·*see	*riqsinakuqmasi*
from	·*mahn·*tah	*-manta*

I'm from Cuzco.
kos·ko·*mahn·*tah *kah·*nee   *Qusqu-manta kani.*

full (after a meal)	sahkh·*sahs·*kah	*saksasqa*
full (complete)	*hoon·*t'ah	*hunt'a*
to have fun	koo·*see·*kui	*kusikuy*
future	*hah·*mokh *pah·*chah	*hamuq pacha*

G

game	pookh·lyai	pukllay
garbage	k'o·pah	q'upa
garden (flower)	pow·kahr	pawqar
garden (fruit)	moo·yah	muya
garlic	ah·hoos	ahus
gate	hai·koo·nah	haykuna
to gather	pah·lyai	pallay
genuine	che·kahkh	chiqaq
to get lost	cheen·kai	chinkay
gift	ree·koo·chee·kui	rikuchikuy
girl	see·pahs	sipas
girlfriend	yah·nah·sah	yanasa
to give	koy	quy
to give birth (humans)	wah·chah·kui	wachakuy
to give birth (animals)	wah·chai	wachay
glass	kes·pee	qispi
to go	ree	riy
to go away	ree·pui	ripuy

> Get lost! Go away!
> *lyokh·see! ree·pui!*   *¡Lluqsiy! ¡Ripuy!*

God	yah·yah	Yaya
gold	ko·ree	quri
good (adj)	ah·lyeen	allin

> Good afternoon.
> *wee·nahs tahr·dees*   *Winas tardis.*
>
> Good evening/night.
> *wee·nahs noo·chees*   *Winas nuchis.*
>
> Good morning.
> *wee·noos dee·yahs*   *Winus diyas.*
>
> Goodbye.
> *teen·koo·nahn·chees·kah·mah*   *Tinkunanchiskama.*

grass	k'ah·choo	q'achu
grave (tomb)	ah·yah sahn·k·hah	aya sankha
great (size)	hah·toon	hatun
great (quality)	koo·sah koo·sah	kusa kusa
to grow	wee·nyai	wiñay
guest	kor·pah	qurpa
guide (person)	nyahn·tah rekh·see·chekh	ñanta riqsichiq

H

hair (of body/animal)	soo·p-hoo	suphu
hair (of head)	chookh·chah	chukcha
half	koos·kahn	kuskan
to halt (oneself)	sah·yai	sayay
to halt (someone else)	sah·yah·chee	sayachiy
handbag	ch'oos·pah	ch'uspa
handsome	soo·mahkh	sumaq
hand-woven	mah·kee·wahn ah·wahs·kah	makiwan awasqa
happy	koo·see • koo·sees·kah	kusi • kusisqa
hard (difficult)	sah·sah	sasa
to have	kai	kay
he	pai	pay
to heal	hahm·pee	hampiy
healer	hahm·pekh	hampiq
health	k-hah·lee kai	qhali kay
to hear	oo·yah·ree	uyariy
to heat	roo·p-hai	ruphay
heaven	hah·nahkh pah·chah	hanaq pacha
heavy	lyah·sah	llasa
to help	yah·nah·pai	yanapay

Help me! yah·nah·pah·wai!		¡Yanapawáy!

---

herb	ko·rah	qura
herbalist	ko·rah·wahn kahm·pekh	qurawan qampiq
here	kai·pee	kaypi

Hey! yow!		¡Yaw!

---

high	soo·nee	suni
hike/to hike	poo·ree	puriy
hill	or·ko·chah	urqucha
to hire	ahl·kee·lai	alkilay
to hold	hah·p'ee	hap'iy
hole	t'o·ko	t'uqu
holiday	p-hees·tah	phista
home	wah·see ai·lyoo	wasi ayllu
honest	soo·mahkh	sumaq
	kow·sai·nee·yokh	kawsayniyuq
honey	ah·nyah·kah	añaka
honeycomb	lah·chee·wah·nah	lachiwana
hope	soo·yai	suyay

horrible	mee·lyai	millay
horse	kah·wah·lyoo	kawallu
to ride a horse	see·lyah·kui	sillakuy
hospital	hahm·pee·nah wah·see	hampina wasi
hot	roo·p·hah	rupha
to be hot (person)	roo·p·hah·ree	ruphariy
house	wah·see	wasi
how	ee·mai·nah	imayna
how much	hai·k'ahn	hayk'an
to hug	mah·k'ah·lyee	mak'alliy
to hug each other	mah·k'ah·lyee·nah·kui	mak'allinakuy
humankind	roo·nah	runa
to be hungry	yahr·kai	yarqay
to hurt	nah·nai	nanay

I

I	no·kah • nyo·kah	nuqa • ñuqa
ice	ch-hoo·lyoon·koo	chhullunku
if	see·choos	sichus
ill	on·kos·kah	unqusqa
to imitate	kah·tee·chee·kui	qatichikuy
immediately	koo·nah·lyahn	kunallan
important	chah·nee·yokh	chaniyuq
in	·pee	-pi
in a hurry	ah·poo·rahs·kah	apurasqa
Inca	een·kah	inka
(to become) infected	ch'oo·pui	ch'upuy
(to become) inflamed	poon·kee	punkiy
to inform	wee·lyai	willay
injury	k'ee·ree	k'iri
inside	oo·k·hoo·pee	ukhupi
instructor	yah·chah·chekh	yachachiq
intelligent	yah·chai·nee·yokh	yachayniyuq
to introduce (a person)	rekh·see·chee	riqsichiy
island	wah·t'ah	wat'a
itch (sensation)	sekh·see	siqsiy

J

jar	oor·poo	urpu
job	lyahn·k'ah·nah	llank'ana
to join	hookh·lyah·kui	hukllakuy
joke	chahn·sah	chansa
to joke	chahn·sah·kui	chansakuy
joker (comedian)	ah·see·chee·kokh	asichikuq

journey	kah·roo poo·ree	karu puriy
juice	hee·lyee	hilli
to jump	p'ee·tai	p'itay
jungle	yoon·kah	yunka

K

to keep	wah·kai·chai	waqaychay
to keep something for someone else	choo·rah·pui	churapuy
key	p'oo·tee • lyah·wee	p'uti • llawi
to kick	hai·t'ai	hayt'ay
to kill	wah·nyoo·chee	wañuchiy
kind (nice)	k-hoo·yah·kokh	khuyakuq
kind (type)	reekh·ch'ahkh	rikch'aq
to kiss	moo·ch'ai	much'ay
kitchen	koo·see·nah	kusina
knapsack	k'e·pee	q'ipi
knife	koo·choo·nah	kuchuna
to know (a fact)	yah·chai	yachay
to know (people or places)	rekh·see	riqsiy

L

lake	ko·chah	qucha
land	ahly·pah	allpa
language	ree·mai • see·mee	rimay • simi
large	hah·toon	hatun
last	kai·nah	qayna
late	tai·ree	tayri
to be late	tai·ree·yai	tayriyay
to laugh	ah·see	asiy
lazy	ke·lyah	qilla
leader	kah·mah·chekh	kamachiq
to lead	poo·sai	pusay
to learn	yah·chai	yachay
leather	kah·rah	qara
to leave (go away)	lyokh·see	lluqsiy
to leave something	sah·kay	saqiy
to be left over (in excess)	poo·chui	puchuy
left (not right)	lyo·k'e	lluq'i
left-handed	lyo·k'en·choo	lluq'inchu
to lend (durable items)	mah·nyai	mañay
to lend (consumables/money)	mah·nui	manuy
to lend a hand	ai·nee	ayniy

letter	*kel*·kah	*qilqa*
liar	*lyoo*·lyah	*llulla*
to lie (be untruthful)	*lyoo*·*lyah*·kui	*llullakuy*
to lie down	*see*·ree	*siriy*
life	*kow*·sai	*kawsay*
light (in weight)	*ch-hah*·lyah	*chhalla*
light (illumination)	*k'ahn*·chai	*k'anchay*
to like	*moo*·nai	*munay*
like (like this)	*hee*·nah	*hina*
liquor	*trah*·woo	*trawu*
to listen	*oo·yah*·ree	*uyariy*
little (small)	*hoo·ch'ui*	*huch'uy*
a little bit	*pee*·see pee·*see*·lyah	*pisi pisilla*
to live	*kow*·sai	*kawsay*
to live in	*tee*·yai	*tiyay*
lock	kahn·dah·*roo*·wahn	*kandaruwan*
	wees·k'ai	*wisq'ay*
to lock	wees·*k'ah*·nah	*wisq'ana*
long (length)	*sui*·t'oo	*suyt'u*
to look/look after	*k-hah*·wai	*qhaway*
to look for	*mahs*·k-hai	*maskhay*
to look like	reekh·*ch'ah*·kui	*rikch'akuy*
loose	*wah*·yah	*waya*
lost	cheen·*kahs*·kah	*chinkasqa*
a lot (quantity)	*ahs*·k-hah	*askha*
love/to love (affection)	*k-hoo*·yai	*khuyay*
love/to love (want/desire)	*moo*·nai	*munay*
love/to love (intense)	*wai*·lyui	*waylluy*
to (be in) love	*son*·ko too·*pah*·chee	*sunqu tupachiy*
to (fall in) love	moo·nah·*nah*·kui	*munanakuy*
to (fall in) love (intense)	wai·lyoo·*nah*·kui	*wayllunakuy*
lover	*moo*·nahkh • *wai*·lyokh	*munaq • waylluq*
luck	*sah*·mee	*sami*
lucky	sah·*mee*·yokh	*samiyuq*
lunch	ahl·*moo*·sai	*almusay*

M

made of	·*mahn*·tah	*-manta*
made of stone	roo·mee·*mahn*·tah	*rumi-manta*
main road	*hah*·toon nyahn	*hatun ñan*
main square	*plah*·sah	*plasa*
to make	*roo*·wai	*ruway*
man	*k-hah*·ree	*qhari*
mankind	*roo*·nah	*runa*
many	*ahs*·k-hah	*askha*

map	*mah*·pah	*mapa*
market	k-*hah*·too • *plah*·sah	*qhatu • plasa*
marriage	kah·sah·*rah*·kui	*kasarakuy*
marvellous	*ahn*·chah soo·mahkh	*ancha sumaq*
Mass (Catholic)	*mee*·sah	*misa*
match (sport)	*pookh*·lyai	*pukllay*
match (to light fires)	foos·*poo*·roo	*phuspuru*
to matter	chah·*nee*·yokh kai	*chaniyuq kay*

> It doesn't matter.
> *mah*·nahn ee·*mah*·nahn·*pahs*·choo   *Manan imananpaschu.*
>
> What's the matter?
> ee·*mah*·tahkh soo·see·dee·*soon*·kee?   *¿Imataq susidisunki?*

mayor	ahl·*kahl*·dee	*alkaldi*
medicine	*hahm*·pee	*hampi*
medium	*tahkh*·sah	*taksa*
to meet	teen·kui	*tinkuy*
to meet up with	*too*·pai	*tupay*
menu	*mee*·noo	*minu*
message	wee·lyah·*chee*·kui	*willachikuy*
middle (in the)	chow·*peen*·pee	*chawpinpi*
milk	*lee*·chee	*lichi*
mirror	*leer*·poo	*lirpu*
to miss (person)	wah·*too*·kui	*watukuy*
mistake (make a)	*pahn*·tai	*pantay*
to mix	*tahkh*·roy	*taqruy*
money	*kol*·ke	*qulqi*
month	*kee*·lyah	*killa*
mosquito net	moos·kee·*tee*·roo	*muskitiru*
moon	*kee*·lyah	*killa*
more	*ahs*·wahn	*aswan*
more or less	*yah*·kah	*yaqa*
much	*ahn*·chah	*ancha*
mud	t'*oo*·roo	*t'uru*
music	moo·*see*·kah	*musika*
musician	moo·*see*·koo	*musiku*

N

name	*soo*·tee	*suti*
to name	soo·*tee*·chai	*sutichay*
narrow	k'*eekh*·lyoo	*k'ikllu*
nation	*lyahkh*·tah	*llaqta*
nature	*kow*·sai *pah*·chah	*kawsay pacha*
near	*sees*·pah • *kai*·lyah	*sispa • qaylla*

neck	*koon·*kah	kunka
necklace	*wahl·*kah	walqa
to need	*moo·*nai	munay
needle (sewing)	ah·*woo·*hah	awuha
needle (large)	*yow·*ree	yawri
neighbour	wah·*see·mah·*see	wasi-masi
never	*mah·*nah hai·*k'ahkh·*pahs	mana hayk'aqpas
new	*moo·*sokh	musuq
news	wee·*lyai·koo·*nah	willaykuna
next (following)	*hah·*mokh • *kah·*tekh	hamuq • qatiq
next to	wahkkh·*tahn·*pee	waqtanpi
nice	ah·*lyeen*	allin
nickname	k-*hoo·*yai *soo·*tee	khuyay suti
night	*too·*tah • *ch'ee·*see	tuta • ch'isi
noise	*rokh·*yah	ruqya
none	*mah·*nah	mana
	ch'oo·*lyah·lyah·*pahs •	ch'ullallapas •
	*mah·*nah *mai·*ken	mana mayqin
north	*wee·*chai	wichay
nothing	*mah·*nahn ee·*mah·*pahs	manan imapas
not yet	mah·*nah·*rahkh	manaraq
now	*koo·*nahn	kunan

O

ocean	ko·*chah·mah·*mah	quchamama
of (poss)	·kh • ·pah	-q • -pa
of course	*ree·*kee	riki
often	nyah·*tahkh·nyah·*tahkh	ñataq-ñataq
old (age)	*mah·*choo	machu
old (worn out)	t-*han·*tah	thanta
on	·pee	-pi

It's on the table.
mee·*sah·*pee *kah·*shahn   *Misa-pi kashan.*

one	hokh	huq
onions	see·*wee·*lyah	siwilla
only	·lyah	-lla
open	kee·*chahs·*kah	kichasqa
to open	*kee·*chai	kichay
opinion	hah·*moo·*t'ai	hamut'ay
or	ee·*chah • oo·*tahkh	icha • utaq
to organise	ah·*lyee·*chai	allichay
original	kahkkh *kee·*keen	kaq kikin
other	hokh	huq

P

Ouch!		
ah·chah·*kow*!		¡Achakáw!

outside	*hah*·wah	hawa
over	*hah*·wahn	hawan
overcoat	p'ees·*too*·nah	p'istuna
to owe (money)	*mah*·noo kai	manu kay
owl	*too*·koo	tuku
owner	*dui*·nyoo	duyñu

P

package	*k'e*·pee	q'ipi
pain	*nah*·nai	nanay
painkillers	*nah*·nai t-ha·*nee*·chekh	nanay thanichiq
to paint	*lyoo*·see	llusiy
painter	*lyoo*·sekh	llusiq
pants	pahn·*tah*·loon	pantalun
paper	*rah*·p'ah • *rah*·p-hee	rap'a • raphi
park	pook·*lyah*·nah *pahm*·pah	pukllana pampa
party	*fees*·tah	phista
to pass (hand to)	*hai*·wai	hayway
to pass (on the street)	*pah*·sai	pasay
to pass (cross a bridge/river)	*cheem*·pai	chimpay
passenger	pah·sah·*hee*·roo	pasahiru
past (remote, undefined time)	*oo*·nai • *nyow*·pah	unay • ñawpa
path	nyahn	ñan
patient (adj)	*lyah*·k·hee	llakhi
to pay	koy • *pah*·gai	quy • pagay
payment	*pah*·goo	pagu
peace	*kah*·see *kow*·sai	qasi kawsay
peak (of a mountain)	*poon*·tah	punta
peas	ahl·*weer*·hahs	alwirhas
pen/pencil	kel·*kah*·nah	qilqana
people	roo·nah·*koo*·nah	runakuna
perhaps	ee·chah·pahs·*chah*	ichapaschá
person	*roo*·nah	runa
pharmacy	hahm·*pee*·yokh *wah*·see	hampiyuq wasi
photo	*foo*·too	phutu
photographer	*foo*·too kor·kokh	phutu qurquq
to pick up (lift)	ho·*kah*·ree	huqariy
to pick up (gather, collect)	*pah*·lyai	pallay

English	Pronunciation	Quechua
piece	*ahkh*·no • *k'ookh*·moo	aqnu • k'ukmu
pill	pahs·*tee*·lyah	pastilla
pillow	*sow*·nah	sawna
place	*pah*·chah	pacha
plane	ah·*wee*·yoon	awiyun
plant	*ko*·rah • *yoo*·rah	qura • yura
to plant (trees)	*mahly*·kee	mallkiy
to plant (sow)	*tahr*·pui	tarpuy
to plant (vegetables)	*yoo*·rai	yuray
plate	*p'oo*·koo	p'uku
to play (games or sport)	*pookh*·lyai	pukllay
to play (music)	wah·*kah*·chee	waqachiy
playing field (sport)	*pookh*·*lyah*·nah	pukllana
	pahm·pah	pampa
plenty	*ahs*·k·hah	askha
pocket	wool·*see*·koo	wulsiku
poem	hah·*rah*·wee	harawi
police	wahr·*dee*·yah	wardiya
pond	*ko*·chah	qucha
poor/poor person	*wahkh*·chah	wakcha
possible	ah·tee·*nah*·lyah	atinalla
pot	*mahn*·kah	manka
pottery	*rahkh*·ch'ee	raqch'i
poverty	*wahkh*·chah kai	wakcha kay
power (ability)	*ah*·tee	atiy
power (strength)	*kahly*·pah	kallpa
powerful (rich/influential)	*k*-hah·pahkh	qhapaq
powerful (dominant)	ah·*tee*·pahkh	atipaq
to pray	mah·*nyah*·kui	mañakuy
to prefer	*moo*·nai	munay
pregnant (humans)	weekh·*sah*·yokh	wiksayuq
pregnant (animals)	*chee*·choo	chichu
to prepare	kah·*mah*·ree	kamariy
present (gift)	ree·k·hoo·*chee*·kui	rikhuchikuy
present (now)	*koo*·nahn • *kah*·nahn	kunan • kanan
pretty	*soo*·mahkh	sumaq
price (fair price)	*chah*·neen	chanin
probably	ee·*chah*·pahs	ichapas
to protect	ah·*mah*·chai	amachay
to pull	*ai*·sai	aysay
pure (water)	*ch'oo*·yah	ch'uya
purse with shoulder strap	*ch'oos*·pah	ch'uspa
to push	*tahn*·kai	tanqay
to put	*choo*·rai	churay

Q

Quechua speakers	roo·nah	runa
Quechua	roo·nah·see·mee	runasimi
question	tah·poo·nah	tapuna
to question	tah·pui	tapuy
quick	p-hah·wahkh • oot·k-hahkh	phawaq • utqhaq
quickly (motion)	p-hah·wai·lyah • oos·k-hai·lyah	phawaylla • usqhaylla
quickly (time)	rah·too·lyah	ratulla
quiet (silence)	ch'een	ch'in
quinoa (Andean grain)	keen·wah • kyoo·nyah	kinwa • kiwña

R

race (contest)	p-hah·wai	phaway
radio	rah·dee·yoo	radiyu
rain	pah·rah	para
to rain	pah·rai	paray
raw (uncooked)	hahn·koo	hanku
to read	lee·yee • nyah·ween·chai	liyiy • ñawinchay
ready	kah·mah·rees·kah	kamarisqa
real (genuine)	che·kahkh	chiqaq
reason	·rai·koo	-rayku
to receive	chahs·kee	chaskiy
recently	chai·rahkh	chayraq
to recognise	rekh·see	riqsiy
to refund	koo·tee·chee·pui	kutichipuy
to refuse	ah·mah nee	ama niy
region	soo·yoo	suyu
to regret	nah·nah·chee·kui	nanachikuy
to reject	ah·mah nee	ama niy
to relax	how·kay	hawkay
to remain	k-he·pai	qhipay
to remember	yoo·yai	yuyay
remote	kah·roo kah·roo	karu karu
to rent	ahl·kee·lai	alkilay
to repeat	koo·tee·pai	kutipay
to respect	yoo·pai·chai	yupaychay
rest/to rest (relax)	sah·mai	samay
rest (remaining)	wah·keen	wakin
restaurant	mee·k-hoo·nah wah·see	mikhuna wasi
restroom	hees·p'ah·koo·nah	hisp'akuna
to return (come back)	koo·tee·mui	kutimuy
rice	ah·roos	arus
to ride (a horse)	see·lyah·kui	sillakuy

right (correct)	chah·neen	chanin
right (not left)	pah·nyah	paña
ring (jewellery)	see·wee	siwi
ripe	po·kos·kah	puqusqa
river	mah·yoo	mayu
road	nyahn	ñan
to rob	soo·wah·kui	suwakuy
rock (stone)	roo·mee	rumi
rope	wahs·k·hah	waskha
round	moo·yoo	muyu
rubbish	k'o·pah	q'upa
rug	kom·pee	qumpi
ruins	nyow·pah lyahkh·tah •	ñawpa llaqta •
	poo·roon lyahkh·tah	purun llaqta
rule	kah·mah·chee	kamachiy
to run	p·hah·wai	phaway

S

sad	lyah·kees·kah	llakisqa
safe	k·hah·lee·lyah	qhalilla
salt	kah·chee	kachi
same	kee·kee	kiki
sand	ah·ko	aqu
to save (a person)	kes·pee·chee	qispichiy
to say	nee	niy
school	yah·chai wah·see	yachay wasi
scissors	koo·choo·nah	kuchuna
sea	ko·chah·mah·mah	quchamama
to search	mahs·k·hai	maskhay
seat	tee·yah·nah	tiyana
to see	k·hah·wai	qhaway
seed	moo·hoo	muhu
to select	ahkh·lyai	akllay
to sell	been·dee	bindiy
to sell at a market/ fair/stand	k·hah·tui	qhatuy
to send a person (on an errand)	kah·chai	kachay
to separate	t'ah·kai • rah·kee	t'aqay • rakiy
to serve food	kah·rai	qaray
to sew	see·rai	siray
shade/shadow	lyahn·t·hoo	llanthu
to shake hands	lyah·mee·yui	llamiyuy
shampoo	chahm·poo	champu
to share one's food/drink	mah·lyee·chee	mallichiy

to shave	p'ahkh·lai	p'aqlay
shawl	lyeekh·lyah	lliklla
she	pai	pay
shelf	choo·rah·ree·nah	churarina
shine	k'ahn·chai	k'anchay
shop	teen·dah	tinda
short	tahkh·sah	taksa
to shout	kah·pah·ree	qapariy
show	k-hah·wah·chee	qhawachiy
shut	wees·k'ahs·kah	wisq'asqa
to shut	wees·k'ai	wisq'ay
sickness/to get sick	on·koy	unquy
side	keen·rai	kinray
sign	oo·nahn·chah	unancha
to sign (a document)	soo·tee sel·k'oy	suti silq'uy
signature	sel·k'o	silq'u
silent	ch'een	ch'in
silver	kol·ke	qulqi
similar	hee·nah	hina
to sing	tah·kee	takiy
singer	tah·kekh	takiq
single man	mah·nah wahr·mee·yokh	mana warmiyuq
single woman	mah·nah qo·sah·yokh	mana qusayuq
single (unique)	ch'oo·lyah	ch'ulla
to sit	tee·yai	tiyay
size/to size	sah·yai	sayay
sky	hah·nahkh pah·chah	hanaq pacha
sky blue	t'okh·rah ahn·kahs	t'uqra anqas
to sleep	poo·nyui	puñuy
sleepy	poo·nyui ai·sai	puñuy aysay
to slide	soo·chui	suchuy
slowly	ah·lyee·lyah·mahn·tah	allillamanta
small	hoo·ch'ui	huch'uy
to smell	moos·k-hee	muskhiy
to smile	ah·see·ree·kui	asirikuy
smoke	q'oos·nyee	q'usñi
to smoke (a cigarette)	pee·tai	pitay
smooth	syookh	siwk
to sneeze	ah·ch-hee	achhiy
snow/to snow	ree·t'ee	rit'i
so	chai hee·nah·kah •	chay hinaqa •
	kai·nah·tah	kaynata
soap	hah·woon	hawun
soft	lyahm·p'oo	llamp'u
solid	ch'ee·lah • choo·choo	ch'ila • chuchu
some (animate object)	wah·keen·koo·nah·lyah	wakinkunalla

some (inanimate object)	wah·kee·wah·kee·lyan	wakiwakillan
someone	pee·pahs	pipas
something	ee·mah·pees • ee·mah·pahs	imapis • imapas
sometimes	mai·nee·lyahn·pee	maynillanpi
song (sad)	tah·kee • hah·rah·wee	taki • harawi
soon	koo·nah·lyan	kunallan

Sorry.
dees·peen·sah·yoo·wai   *Dispinsayuway.*

sound	sui·nai	suynay
Spanish	kahs·tee·lyah·noo	kastillanu
to speak	ree·mai	rimay
speedy	oos·k-hakh	usqhaq
spindle (for spinning)	poos·kah	puska
spring (water)	pookh·yoo	pukyu
square (shape)	tah·wah k'oo·choo·yokh	tawa k'uchuyuq
square (town)	plah·sah	plasa
stairs	pah·tah pah·tah	pata pata
to stand	sah·yai	sayay
stars	koy·lyoor • ch'ahs·kah	quyllur • ch'aska
to start	kah·lyah·ree	qallariy
to stay (remain)	k-he·pai	qhipay
to steal	soo·wai	suway
steam	wahkh·see	waksi
steep	sah·yahkh	sayaq
to step	t-haht·kee	thatkiy
step on	sah·rui	saruy
stone	roo·mee	rumi
to stop (oneself)	sah·yai	sayay
to stop (someone else)	sah·yah·chee	sayachiy
storm	lyokh·lyahh pah·rah	lluqlla para
story	wee·lyah·kui	willakuy
straight	syook	siwk
stranger	mah·nah rek·sees·kah	mana riqsisqa
stream	mah·yoo·chah • oo·noo hai·kokh	mayucha • unu haykuq
street	nyahn • kah·lyee	ñan • kalli
strength	kahly·pah	kallpa
string	k'ai·too	q'aytu
strong (solid)	choo·choo	chuchu
strong (durable)	kah·kah	qaqa
strong (person)	seen·chee	sinchi
student	yah·chai moo·nahkh	yachay munaq

stupid	mah·nah ah·lyeen yoo·yai·nee·yokh	mana allin yuyayniyuq
to succeed	ah·lyeen·wahn lyokh·see	allinwan lluqsiy
to suffer	nyah·kai	ñakay
sugar	mees·k'ee • ah·soo·kahr	misk'i • asukar
suitcase	mah·lee·tah	malita
sunlight	roo·p·hai	ruphay
sunrise	een·tee lyee·pee·pee·mui • lyokh·see·mui	inti llipipimuy • lluqsimuy
sunset	ch'ee·see·yai·pui • een·tee·yai·kui	ch'isiyapuy • intiyaykuy
to sweep	pee·chai	pichay
sweet	mees·k'ee	misk'i
to swim	wai·t'ai	wayt'ay

T

table	wahm·pahr	wampar
to take	ah·pai	apay
to take (on your back)	k'e·pee	q'ipiy
talk	ree·mai	rimay
tall	hah·toon	hatun
tambourine	teen·yah	tinya
to taste	mah·lyee	malliy
tasty	soo·mahkh • mees·k'ee	sumaq • misk'i
teacher	yah·chah·chekh • hah·mow·t'ah	yachachiq • hamawt'a
tear	we·ke	wiqi
teeth	kee·roo	kiru
to tell	nee • wee·lyai	niy • willay
temperature (fever)	roo·p·hai on·koy	ruphay unquy
temple	mahn·ko/yoo·pai·chai wah·see	manqu/yupaychay wasi
terrible	mah·nah ah·lyeen	mana allin
to thank	ah·nyai·chai • sool·pai nee	añaychay • sulpáy niy

Thank you.
ah·nyai·chai·kee • sool·pai   Añaychayki. • Sulpáy.

that	chai • ahn·chai	chay • anchay
that over there	chah·hai • hah·kai	chahay • haqay
them	pai·koo·nah	paykuna
then (at that time)	chai pah·chah	chay pacha
there	chai·pee	chaypi
they	pai·koo·nah	paykuna

thief	*soo·*wah	suwa
thin (skinny)	*too·*lyoo	tullu
to think	*yoo·*yai	yuyay
thirst	*ch'ah·*kee	ch'akiy
thirsty	*ch'ah·kees·*kah	ch'akisqa
this	kai	kay
thought	*yoo·*yai	yuyay
to tie	*wah·*tai	watay
tight	*mah·t'ee*	mat'i
time	*pah·*chah	pacha
tin (of food)	*lah·*tah	lata
tin opener	*lah·tah kee·chah·*nah	lata kichana
tired	*sai·k'oos·*kah	sayk'usqa
today	*koo·nahn p'oon·*chai	kunan p'unchay
together	*koos·*kah	kuska
toilet	*hees·p'ah·koo·*nah	hisp'akuna
tomorrow	*pah·kah·*reen	paqarin
too	·pees • ·pahs	-pis • -pas

Me too.
no·*kah·*pees•   *Nuqa-pis.•*
nyo·*kah·*pahs   *Ñuqa-pas.*

too much	*chee·kah chee·*kah	chika chika
torch	*k'ahn·chah·*nah	k'anchana
to touch	*lyah·*mee	llamiy
tourist	*too·rees·*tah	turista
towards/to	·mahn • ·tah	-man • -ta
towel	*too·wah·*lyah	tuwalla
town	*lyahkh·*tah	llaqta
track (path)	nyahn	ñan
to translate	*t'eekh·*rai	t'ikray
trash	*k'o·*pah	q'upa
to travel	*ch'oo·*sai • *poo·*ree	ch'usay • puriy
traveller	*poo·*rekh	puriq
tree	*mahly·*kee	mallki
to trek	*kah·roo poo·*ree	karu puriy
truck	*kah·mee·*yoon	kamiyun
true	*che·*kahkh	chiqaq

It's true!
che·*kahkh·*mee!   *¡Chiqaqmi!*

to trust	*koon·p·hee·*yai	kunphiyay
truth	*che·*kahkh	chiqaq

to turn	moo·yoo·ree	muyuriy

> Turn left.
> lyo·k'e·mahn moo·yoo·ree — *Lluq'iman muyuriy.*
>
> Turn right.
> pah·nyah·mahn moo·yoo·ree — *Pañaman muyuriy.*

twice	*ees*·kai *koo*·tee	*iskay kuti*

U

under	*pah*·chahn	*pachan*
to understand	een·*teen*·dee	*intindiy*
universe	tekh·see·*moo*·yoo	*tiqsimuyu*
until	·*kah*·mah	*-kama*
up	hah·nahkh	*hanaq*
uphill	*wee*·chai	*wichay*
to be upset	p-hee·*nyah*·kui	*phiñakuy*
urgent	oos·*k-hai*·pahkh	*usqhaypaq*
useful	*ah*·lyeen	*allin*

V

vacation	*sah*·mai *pah*·chah	*samay pacha*
valley	k-hes·wah • *wai*·k'o	*qhiswa • wayq'u*
valuable	chah·nee·yokh	*chaniyuq*
value	*chah*·neen	*chanin*
vegetarian	*mah*·nah *ai*·chah	*mana aycha*
	mee·kokh	*mikuq*
very	*ahn*·chah	*ancha*
village	*lyahkh*·tah	*llaqta*
to visit	wah·*too*·kui	*watukuy*

W

to wait	*soo*·yai	*suyay*
to walk	*poo*·ree	*puriy*
wall	*per*·kah	*pirqa*
to want	*moo*·nai	*munay*
warm	*k'o*·nyee	*q'uñi*
to warm up	*k'o*·nyee·kui	*q'uñikuy*
to warn	yoo·*yahm*·pai	*yuyampay*
to wash (clothes/hair)	*t'ahkh*·sai	*t'aqsay*
to wash (general, except clothes/hair)	*mahkh*·ch-hee	*maqchhiy*
to wash oneself (bathe)	ahr·*mah*·kui	*armakuy*

ENGLISH – QUECHUA DICTIONARY

W

washing powder	dee·teer·*heen*·tee	*ditirhinti*
watch	k-*hah*·wai	*qhaway*
to watch	ree·looh	*riluh*
water	oo·noo • *yah*·koo	*unu • yaku*
waterfall	p-hahkh·chah	*phaqcha*
way (path)	nyahn	*ñan*
we (exclusive)	no·kai·koo	*nuqayku*
we (inclusive)	no·kahn·chees	*nuqanchis*
weak	*kahly*·pah wah·nyui	*kallpa wañuy*
to wear (clothes)	p'ah·chah·*lyee*·kui	*p'achallikuy*
to weave	ah·wai	*away*
wedding	kah·sah·*rah*·kui	*kasarakuy*
week	see·*mah*·nah	*simana*
to weigh	ai·sai	*aysay*
weight	*lyah*·sah	*llasa*
well	ah·lyeen	*allin*
west	een·tee cheen·*kai*·kui	*inti chinkaykuy*
wet	ho·k'o	*huq'u*

What? ee·mahn?		¿*Iman?*
What! (response to being called) hai!/ee·mah!		¡Hay!/¡Ima!
When? hai·k'ahkh?		¿Hayk'aq?
Where? mai·peen?		¿Maypin?
From where? mai·*mahn*·tahn?		¿Maymantan?
To where? mai·*tah*·tahkh?		¿Maytataq?
Which? mai·keen?		¿Mayqin?
Who? peen? (sg)/pee·*koo*·nahn? (pl)		¿Pin?/¿Pikunan?
Who is it? peen?		¿Pin?
Whose? pekh·pah?		¿Piqpa?
Why? ee·mah·*nahkh*·teen?		¿Imanaqtin?

D I C T I O N A R Y

197

window	t'o·ko • ween·tah·nah	t'uqu • wintana
winter	chee·ree mee·t'ah	chiri mit'a
with	·wahn	-wan
with me	no·kah·wahn	nuqa-wan
woman	wahr·mee	warmi
wonderful	ahn·chah soo·mahkh	ancha sumaq
wood	k'oo·lyoo	k'ullu
wool	meely·mah	millma
word	ree·mai • see·mee	rimay • simi
to work	lyahn·k'ai	llank'ay
world	pah·chah •	pacha •
	tekh·see·moo·yoo	tiqsimuyu
worried	lyah·kees·kah	llakisqa
to worship	yoo·pai·chai	yupaychay
worth (value)	chah·neen	chanin
to write	kel·kai	qilqay
wrong (mistaken)	pahn·tah	panta

Y

year	wah·tah	wata
you (sg)	kahn	qan
you (pl)	kahn·koo·nah	qankuna

Z

| zero | ch'oo·sahkh | ch'usaq |

A

achhiy	ah·ch-hee	to sneeze
aha	ah·hah	*chicha* (maize beer)
ahinaqa	ah·hee·*nah*·kah	so
akllay	*ahk*·lyai	to choose
aksidinti	ahkh·see·*deen*·tee	accident
akupana	ah·koo·*pah*·nah	sunset
alkaldi	ahl·*kahl*·dee	mayor
alkilay	ahl·*kee*·lai	to hire • to rent
almusay	ahl·*moo*·sai	to have lunch
allillamanta	ah·lyee·lyah·*mahn*·tah	slowly
allin	ah·lyeen	good • useful • well
allpa	*ahly*·pah	land • earth (soil)
ama niy	ah·mah nee	to refuse • to reject
amachay	ah·*mah*·chai	to protect
amisqa	ah·*mes*·kah	bored • boring
ancha	ahn·chah	much • very
apamuy	ah·*pah*·mui	to bring
apay	ah·pai	to take
apu	ah·poo	rich
apurasqa	ah·poo·*rahs*·kah	in a hurry
aqnu	*ahkh*·no	piece
aqu	ah·ko	sand
armakuy	ahr·*mah*·kui	to bathe • to wash oneself
arpha	ahr·p-hah	blind (adj)
as aslla	ahs *ahs*·lyah	a little bit
asirikuy	ah·see·*ree*·kui	to smile
asiti	ah·*see*·tee	oil (cooking)
asiy	*ah*·see	to laugh
askamalla	ahs·kah·*mah*·lyah	quickly • fast (time)
askha	*ahs*·k-hah	many • a lot of
asnay	ahs·nai	to smell
asukar	ah·*soo*·kahr	sugar
aswan	*ahs*·wahn	more
aswan allin	*ahs*·wahn ah·lyeen	better
aswan hatun	*ahs*·wahn hah·toon	bigger
atinalla	ah·tee·*nah*·lyah	possible
atipaq	ah·*tee*·pahkh	powerful
atipay	ah·*tee*·pai	to put up with
atiy	*ah*·tee	to be able • power • strength
away	ah·wai	to weave
awiyun	ah·*wee*·yoon	aeroplane
awtu	*ow*·too	car
awuha	ah·*woo*·hah	needle (sewing)
aya p'ampana	ah·yah p'ahm·*pah*·nah	cemetery
aya sankha	*ah*·yah *sahn*·k-hah	grave • tomb
aycha kurku	ai·chah *koor*·koo	body

ayllu	ai·lyoo	community • family
ayniy	ai·nee	to help out
ayqi	ai·ke	to exit • to leave
aysay	ai·sai	to pull • to stretch

B

bañu	bah·nyoo	bathroom • toilet
bindiy	been·dee	to sell

CH

chahay	chah·hai	that over there
chaka	chah·kah	bridge • thigh
chakra	chahkh·rah	farm • field (cultivated) • earth (soil)
chanin	chah·neen	fair price • value • worth • right • correct • true
chaniyuq	chah·nee·yokh	important • valuable
chaniyuq kay	chah·nee·yokh kai	to matter (be important)
chansa	chahn·sah	joke
chaskiy	chahs·kee	to receive
chawpinpi	chow·peen·pee	in the middle
chay	chai	that
chay hinaqa	chai hee·nah·kah	so
chay pacha	chai pah·chah	then • at that time
chayasqa	chah·yahs·kah	done (of food)
chayay	chai·yai	to arrive
chayllaña	chai·lyah·nyah	enough
chaymanta	chai·mahn·tah	besides (furthermore)
chaymantaqa	chai·mahn·tah·kah	afterwards
chaypachamanta	chai·pah·chah·mahn·tah	since then
chaypas	chai·pahs	although
chaypi	chai·pee	there
chayraq	chai·rahkh	recently
chimpapi	cheem·pah·pee	across (from)
chimpay	cheem·pai	to pass • to cross over
chinkasqa	cheen·kahs·kah	lost • hidden
chipchiy	cheep·chee	to shine (sun) • to illuminate
chiqanta	che·kahn·tah	straight
chiqaq	che·kahkh	truth • real • genuine
chiskasqa puriy	chees·kahs·kah poo·ree	to be lost
chiyay	chee·yai	to arrive
chuchu	choo·choo	solid • strong
chupi	choo·pee	soup
churanakuy	choo·rah·nah·kui	to argue
churapuy	choo·rah·pui	to keep something for someone else
churarina	choo·rah·ree·nah	shelf

churay	choo·rai	to put • to inject
chusi	choo·see	blanket
chuyk'ucha	chui·k'oo·chah	cup

CHH

chhalay	ch-hah·lai	to barter • to exchange
chhalla	ch-hah·lyah	light (in weight)
chhika	ch-hee·kah	plenty
chhika chhika	ch-hee·kah ch-hee·kah	too much • too many
chhulli	ch-hoo·lyee	influenza
chhullunku	ch-hoo·lyoon·koo	ice
chhuqay	ch-ho·kai	to push

CH'

ch'aka	ch'ah·kah	sore throat • hoarse
ch'aki	ch'ah·kee	dry
ch'akisqa	ch'ah·kees·kah	thirsty
ch'akiy	ch'ah·kee	to dry • to be thirsty • thirst
ch'aska	ch'ahs·kah	stars
ch'ikay	ch'ee·kai	sting (of bee/wasp)
ch'in	ch'een	quiet (silence) • silent
ch'iqmiy	ch'ekh·mee	to bother
ch'isiyay	ch'ee·see·yai	to get dark
ch'ulla	ch'oo·lyah	single (unique)
ch'unku	ch'oon·koo	crowd • group
ch'upuy	ch'oo·pui	to become infected
ch'usaq	ch'oo·sahkh	space • zero • empty
ch'usay	ch'oo·sai	to travel
ch'uspa	ch'oos·pah	small bag • handbag
ch'ustikuy	ch'oos·tee·kui	to undress
ch'uya	ch'oo·yah	clean • pure (of water)

D

| Diyus | dee·yoos | God |
| duktur | dookh·toor | doctor |

H

hamawt'a	hah·mow·t'ah	teacher • professor • community leader • wise
hampi	hahm·pee	drug • medicine
hampina wasi	hahm·pee·nah wah·see	hospital
hampiq	hahm·pekh	healer
hampiy	hahm·pee	to heal • to cure
hampiyuq wasi	hahm·pee·yokh wah·see	drugstore • pharmacy

hamuq	hah·mokh	next (following)
hamuy	hah·mui	to come
hanaq	hah·nahkh	up • above
hanaq pacha	hah·nahkh pah·chah	heaven • sky
hanku	hahn·koo	raw (uncooked)
hanq'ara	hahn·k'ah·rah	dish
hap'iy	hah·p'ee	to hold
haqay	hah·kai	that over there
harawi	hah·rah·wee	poem • song
hark'apay	hahr·k'ah·pai	to protect
hark'ay	hahr·k'ai	to prevent
hasp'ikuy	hahs·p'ee·kui	itch • to scratch
hatun	hah·toon	big • high • large • tall
hawa	hah·wah	outside
hawa runa	hah·wah roo·nah	foreigner
hawanpi	hah·wahn·pee	above
hawan	hah·wahn	over
hawapi	hah·wah·pee	outside
hawkay	how·kai	to relax
hayk'an	hai·k'ahn	how much
hayk'aq	hai·k'ahkh	when
haykuna	hai·koo·nah	gate
haykuy	hai·kui	to enter
hayway	hai·wai	to pass (hand to)
hina	hee·nah	similar • like this/that
hina kaqlla	hee·nah kahkh·lyah	permanent
hinaspa	hee·nahs·pah	besides (furthermore) • thus
hinastin	hee·nahs·teen	everywhere
hisp'akuna	hees·p'ah·koo·nah	toilet • restroom
hisp'akuy	hees·p'ah·kui	to urinate
hucha	hoo·chah	fault • sin
huchallikuy	hoo·chah·lyee·kui	to sin
huch'uy	hoo·ch'ui	small • little
huk'i	hoo·k'ee	corner (inside)
huklla	hookh·lyah	together
hukllakuy	hookh·lyah·kui	to join
hukllay	hookh·lyai	to mix
hunt'a	hoon·t'ah	full (complete)
hunt'asqa	hoon·t'ahs·kah	exact • exactly
huñiy	hoo·nyee	to allow • to permit
hup'a	hoo·p'ah	deaf
huq	hokh	one • another • other
huq ratuña	hokh rah·too·nyah	ago
huqariy	ho·kah·ree	to pick up (lift)
huqmanta	hokh·mahn·tah	again
huqnirayay	hokh·nee·rah·yai	to change (into something) • to become
huq'u	ho·k'o	damp • wet
hurquy	hor·koy	to take

I

icha	*ee·chah*	or
ichapas	*ee·chah·pahs*	probably
ichapaschá	*ee·chah·pahs·chah*	perhaps
imallapas	*ee·mah·lyah·pahs*	anything • something
iman	*ee·mahn*	what
imanaqtin	*ee·mah·nahkh·teen*	why
imayna	*ee·mai·nah*	how
iniy/iñiy	*ee·nee/ee·nyee*	to believe (religious)
inka	*een·kah*	Inca
inlis	*een·lees*	English
inlisa	*een·lee·sah*	church
intindiy	*een·teen·dee*	to understand
isanka	*ee·sahn·kah*	basket
iskay kuti	*ees·kai koo·tee*	twice
iskaynin	*ees·kai·neen*	both

K

kachay	*kah·chai*	to send (on an errand)
kalli	*kah·lyee*	street
kallpa	*kahly·pah*	strength
kallpa wañuy	*kahly·pah wah·nyui*	weak
-kama	*·kah·mah*	until
kamachiy	*kah·mah·chee*	to order • to rule
kamarikuy	*kah·mah·ree·kui*	to decide
kamarisqa	*kah·mah·rees·kah*	ready
kamariy	*kah·mah·ree*	to prepare
kambiyay	*kahm·bee·yai*	to change
kamisa	*kah·mee·sah*	shirt
kanallan	*kah·nah·lyahn*	immediately • very soon
kanasta	*kah·nahs·tah*	basket
kandaruwan wisq'ay	*kahn·dah·roo·wahn wees·k'ai*	to lock
kaniy	*kah·nee*	bite (of any creature)
kaq kikin	*kahkh kee·keen*	original
karu	*kah·roo*	far
karu llaqta	*kah·roo lyahkh·tah*	abroad
karu llaqta runa	*kah·roo lyahkh·tah roo·nah*	foreigner
karu puriy	*kah·roo poo·ree*	journey • trek
karru	*kah·rroo*	car • truck
kasarakuqmasi	*kah·sah·rah·kokh·mah·see*	fiancé • fiancée
kasarakuy	*kah·sah·rah·kui*	to marry • marriage • wedding
kastillanu	*kahs·tee·lyah·noo*	Spanish
katuliku	*kah·too·lee·koo*	Catholic

kawra	*kow*·rah	goat
kawsay pacha	*kow*·sai *pah*·chah	nature
kay	kai	to exist • to be • to have • this
kaynata	kai·*nah*·tah	so
kaypi	*kai*·pee	here
kichasqa	kee·*chahs*·kah	open
kichay	*kee*·chai	to open
kiki	*kee*·kee	same
killa	*kee*·lyah	month • moon
kinray	*keen*·rai	side
kinwa	*keen*·wah	quinoa (Andean grain)
kirpu	*keer*·poo	body
kuchuna	koo·*choo*·nah	knife • scissors
kuchuy	koo·chui	to cut
kunallan	koo·*nah*·lyan	immediately • very soon
kunan	koo·nahn	now • present (now)
kunan pacha	koo·nahn *pah*·chah	right now
kunphiyay	koon·p·*hee*·yai	to trust
kuntra	*koon*·trah	against
kura	*koo*·rah	priest
kurku	*koor*·koo	body
kusa	*koo*·sah	nice • right (interjection)
kusa kusa	*koo*·sah *koo*·sah	great (quality) • marvellous • wonderful
kusi	*koo*·see	happy
kusikuy	koo·*see*·kui	to have fun
kusisqa	koo·*sees*·kah	happy
kuska	*koos*·kah	side by side • together
kuskachakuy	koos·kah·*chah*·kui	to join
kutichipuy	koo·tee·*chee*·pui	to refund • compensation
kutichiy	koo·*tee*·chee	to answer
kutimuy	koo·*tee*·mui	to return (come back)
kutipay	koo·*tee*·pai	to repeat
kutuna	*koo*·*too*·*nah*	jacket (of a woman)
kwistay	*kwees*·tai	to cost

KH

khachuy	k·*hah*·chui	to bite (dog) • to bite off
kharka	k·*hahr*·kah	dirty
khumpa	k·*hoom*·pah	friend
khutu	k·*hoo*·too	frozen (solid)
khuyakuq	k·hoo·*yah*·kəkh	kind (nice)
khuyay	k·*hoo*·yai	love/to love
khuyay suti	k·*hoo*·yai *soo*·tee	nickname

QUECHUA – ENGLISH DICTIONAR

K'

k'akra	k'ahk·rah	ceramic
k'allma	k'ahly·mah	branch
k'anay	k'ah·nai	to burn • to set fire to
k'anchay	k'ahn·chai	to shine (sun) • to illuminate • light
k'apak	k'ah·pahkh	exact • exactly
k'aphra	k'ah·p-hrah	ceramic
k'awchi	k'ow·chee	jar
k'ikllu	k'eek·lyoo	narrow
k'iri	k'ee·ree	injury • wound
k'irikuy	k'ee·ree·kui	to wound
k'uchu	k'oo·choo	corner (outside)
k'ukmu	k'ookh·moo	piece
k'uku	k'oo·koo	short (in distance)
k'utuy	k'oo·tui	bite (insect) • to bite (hard things)

L

laranha	lah·rahn·hah	orange (fruit)
lata	lah·tah	can (of food)
lata kichana	lah·tah kee·chah·nah	can opener
lawa	lah·wah	soup
lintirna	leen·teer·nah	torch • flashlight
lirpu	leer·poo	mirror
liyiy	lee·yee	to read
lus	loos	electric light
luylu	lui·loo	clean

LL

-lla	·lyah	only
llakhi	lyah·k-hee	patient
llakisqa	lyah·kees·kah	sad • worried
llakllay	lyahkh·lyai	to sense • to feel
llamiy	lyah·mee	to feel (touch)
llamiyuy	lyah·mee·yui	to shake hands
llamp'u	lyahm·p'oo	soft
llank'ana	lyahn·k'ah·nah	job
llanthu	lyahn·t-hoo	shade • shadow
llapa	lyah·pah	everything • every • all
llapan	lyah·pahn	everyone
llapanku	lyah·pahn·koo	everyone
llaqta	lyahkh·tah	city • community • country • nation • town • village

llasa	lyah·sah	heavy • weight
llimpi	lyeem·pee	colour
lliw	lyoo	every • all • everything
lliwninku	lyoo·neen·koo	everyone
llulla	lyoo·lyah	liar
llullakuy	lyoo·lyah·kui	to lie (be untruthful)
llumpaq	lyoom·pahkh	pure • innocent
llumpay sumaq	lyoom·pai soo·mahkh	wonderful
llunch'iq	lyoon·ch'ekh	painter
lluq'i	lyo·k'e	left (not right)
lluq'inchu	lyo·k'en·choo	left-handed
lluqsiy	lyokh·see	to depart • to exit • to go away
llusiy	lyoo·see	to colour • to paint

M

machasqa/machaq	mah·chahs·kah/ mah·chahkh	drunk
machu	mah·choo	old (age)
machay	mah·chai	to get drunk
mahanakuy	mah·kah·nah·kui	fight • to fight
makiwan awasqa	mah·kee·wahn ah·wahs·kah	hand-woven
mak'allinakuy	mah·k'ah·lyee·nah·kui	to hug each other
mak'alliy	mah·k'ah·lyee	to hug
mak'as	mah·k'ahs	jar
malita	mah·lee·tah	luggage • suitcase
malqu	mahl·ko	chick
malliy	mah·lyee	to taste
malliyachiy	mah·lyee·yah·chee	to share one's food • to drink with someone
mallki mallki	mahly·kee mahly·kee	forest
mallkiy	mahly·kee	to plant
mama	mah·mah	mother • Mrs • Madam
-man	·mahn	towards • to
mana allin	mah·nah ah·lyeen	bad •
mana allin yuyayniyuq	mah·nah ah·lyeen yoo·yai·nee·yuq	stupid
mana mayqin	mah·nah mai·ken	none
mana qasiq	mah·nah kah·sekh	busy
mana qusayuq	mah·nah koo·sah·yokh	single woman
mana riqsisqa	mah·nah rek·sees·kah	stranger
mana warmiyuq	mah·nah wahr·mee·yokh	single man
manan imapas	mah·nahn ee·mah·pahs	nothing

manan niy	mah·nahn nee	to deny
manaraq	mah·nah·rahkh	not yet
manchakuy	mahn·chah·kui	to be afraid • fear
manchay	mahn·chai	danger
manka	mahn·kah	pan • pot
-manta	·mahn·tah	from • made of
manu kay	mah·noo kai	to owe (money)
manuy	mah·nui	to lend (consumables/money)
mañakuy	mah·nyah·kui	to ask (for something) • to borrow • to pray
mañay	mah·nyai	to lend (durable items)
map'a	mah·p'ah	awful
maqanakuy	mah·kah·nah·kui	to argue
maqchhiy	mahkh·ch·hee	to wash (general, not clothes/hair)
masi	mah·see	companion • member (club)
maskhay	mahs·k·hai	to look for • to search
mat'i	mah·t'ee	tight
mat'isqa	mah·t'ees·kah	tight
maypin	mai·peen	where
maymantan	mai·mahn·tahn	from where
maytataq	mai·tah·tahkh	to where
mayqin	mai·keen	which
michiy	mee·chee	to pasture
mihuy	mee·hui	to eat • food • lunch
mikhuna wasi	mee·k-hoo·nah wah·see	restaurant
mik'i	mee·k'ee	slightly damp
millay	mee·lyai	ugly
millay millay	mee·lyai mee·lyai	horrible (appearance)
misa	mee·sah	Mass (Catholic worship service)
misk'i	mees·k'ee	sweet • delicious • tasty • honey • sugar
much'ay	moo·ch'ai	to kiss • to worship
muhu	moo·hoo	seed
munakuq	moo·nah·kokh	kind (nice)
munanakuy	moo·nah·nah·kui	to love (fall in)
munay	moo·nai	love • to love • to want • to desire • to prefer
munaq	moo·nahkh	lover
muskhiy	moos·k-hee	to smell
musqhuy	mos·k-hoy	dream • to dream
musuq	moo·sokh	new
muya	moo·yah	garden (fruit)
muyu	moo·yoo	round
muyuriy	moo·yoo·ree	to turn

N

nanachikuy	nah·nah·chee·kui	to regret • to resent
nanay	nah·nai	to hurt • physical pain
nanay thaniciq	nah·nai t-ha·nee·chekh	painkillers
naqha	nah·k·hah	ago
niy	nee	to say • to tell

Ñ

-ña	·nyah	already
ñakay	nyah·kai	to suffer
ñakariy	nyah·kah·ree	to suffer
ñan	nyahn	path • road • way
ñaña	nyah·nyah	friend (female friend to female) • sister (of woman)
ñanta riqsichiq	nyahn·tah rekh·see·chekh	guide (person)
ñapu	nyah·poo	ripe
ñaqch'a	nyahkh·ch'ah	comb
ñaqha	nyah·k·hah	ago
ñawinchay	nyah·ween·chai	to read
ñawpa	nyow·pah	past • ancient
ñawpa llaqta	nyow·pah lyahkh·tah	ruins
ñawpaq	nyow·pahkh	ahead • past • ancient
ñawpaq kaq	nyow·pahkh kahkh	first
ñawpaqta	nyow·pahkh·tah	before (time)
ñawsa	nyow·sah	blind (adj)
ñiqin	nyeh·ken	first

P

-pa	·pah	of
pacha	pah·chah	world • universe • space • time
pacha kuyuy	pah·chah koo·yui	earthquake
pacha phuyu	pah·chah p-hoo·yoo	fog
pachan	pah·chahn	under
pagu	pah·goo	payment
pallay	pah·lyai	to pick up • to collect
pampa	pahm·pah	countryside • flat place • floor • plain
pampachay	pahm·pah·chai	to forgive
pana/pani	pah·nah/pah·nee	friend (female friend to male) • sister (of man)
panta	pahn·tah	wrong • mistaken
pantalun	pahn·tah·loon	trousers
pantay	pahn·tai	to make a mistake

paña	*pah·nyah*	right (not left)
paqta	*pahkh·tah*	perhaps
para	*pah·rah*	rain
pasahiru	*pah·sah·hee·roo*	passenger
pasaq kutilla	*pah·sahkh koo·tee·lyah*	constantly • always
pasay	*pah·sai*	to pass (on the street)
pasayuy	*pah·sah·yui*	to enter
pastilla	*pahs·tee·lyah*	pill
pata	*pah·tah*	over • on
patapi	*pah·tah·pee*	above
phukuna waqra	*p-hoo·koo·nah wahkh·rah*	Andean horn
pin	*peen*	who
-pi	*·pee*	on • in • at
pichay	*pee·chai*	to clean • to sweep
pikaq	*pee·kahkh*	scorpion
piluta	*pee·loo·tah*	ball
pipas	*pee·pahs*	someone
piqpa	*pekh·pah*	whose
pirqa	*per·kah*	wall
pirqachay	*per·kah·chai*	to build
-pis	*·pees*	also • too • and
pisi	*pee·see*	few • little • scarce
pisi pisilla	*pee·see pee·see·lyah*	a little bit
pitay	*pee·tai*	to smoke (a cigarette)
plasa	*plah·sah*	plaza
prisisaqpaq	*pree·see·sahkh·pahkh*	urgent
puchuy	*poo·chui*	be left over (excess)
pukara	*poo·kah·rah*	fort • fortress
pukllana pampa	*pook·lyah·nah pahm·pah*	park • playing field
pukllapayay	*pook·lyah·pah·yai*	to make fun of
pukllay	*pookh·lyai*	to play (game/sport) • game • match (sport)
pukyu	*pook·yoo*	spring (water)
punta	*poon·tah*	peak (mountain)
puñuna	*poo·nyoo·nah*	bed
puñuy	*poo·nyui*	to sleep
puñuy aysay	*poo·nyui ai·sai*	sleepy
puqusqa	*po·kos·kah*	ripe
puquy	*po·koy*	to produce
puriq	*poo·rekh*	traveller
puriy	*poo·ree*	to hike • to walk • to travel • trip
purun llaqta	*poo·roon lyahkh·tah*	ruins
pusamuy	*poo·sah·mui*	to fetch
pusaq	*poo·sahkh*	guide (person)
pusay	*poo·sai*	to lead • to guide
puskay	*poos·kai*	to spin (thread)

PH

phasil	fah·seel	easy
phawaq	p-hah·wahkh	quick
phaway	p-hah·wai	to fly • to run • race
phawariy	p-hah·wah·ree	to run
phawaylla	p-hah·wai·lyah	fast (movement) • quickly
phiña	p-hee·nyah	angry
phistihay	fees·tee·hai	to celebrate
phukuy	p-hoo·kui	to play (music)
phuspuru	p-hoos·poo·roo	match (to light fires)

P'

p'acha	p'ah·chah	dress • clothes
p'achallikuy	p'ah·chah·lyee·kui	to wear clothes • to dress oneself
p'akisqa	p'ah·kees·kah	broken
p'akiy	p'ah·kee	to break
p'alta	p'ahl·tah	flat
p'inqasqa	p'en·kahs·kah	embarrassed
p'itay	p'ee·tai	to jump
p'uchukay	p'oo·choo·kai	to finish
p'uku	p'oo·koo	dish • plate
p'uti	p'oo·tee	key • lock

Q

-q	·kh	of
qallariy	kah·lyah·ree	to begin • to start
qanra	kahn·rah	dirty
qaparqachay	kah·pahr·kah·chai	to scream
qaqa	kah·kah	cliff • stone • rock • strong • durable
qara	kah·rah	leather • skin
qaray	kah·rai	to serve food • to feed
qasa	kah·sah	ice
qasay	kah·sai	to freeze
qasi kawsay	kah·see kow·sai	peace
qata	kah·tah	blanket
qatichikuy	kah·tee·chee·kui	to copy
qatiq	kah·tekh	next • following • descendant
qatiy	kah·tee	to follow
qaylla	kai·lyah	near
qayna	kai·nah	last
qayqa	kai·kah	crazy
qilla	ke·lyah	lazy

qilqa	kel·kah	letter
qilqana	kel·kah·nah	pen • pencil
qilqay	kel·kai	to write
qincha	ken·chah	fence
qiru	ke·ro	cup (ceremonial, of the Incas)
qispi	kes·pee	crystal • glass • free (at liberty)
qulqisapa	kol·ke·sah·pah	rich
qunqay	kon·kai	to forget
qura	ko·rah	herb • plant
qurawan qampiq	ko·rah·wahn kahm·pekh	herbalist
quri	ko·ree	gold
qurpa	kor·pah	guest
qurpa wasi	kor·pah wah·see	accommodation
qurpachana	kor·pah·chah·nah	accommodation
quy	koy	to give • to pay
quya	ko·yah	queen
quykuy	koy·kui	to pay
quyllur	koy·lyoor	stars

QH

qhali kay	k-hah·lee kai	health
qhalilla	k-hah·lee·lyah	safe
qhampu	k-hahm·poo	spider
qhapaq	k-hah·pahkh	powerful • rich
qhapiru	k-hah·pee·roo	band
qhaqllin	k-hahkh·lyeen	jaw (lower)
qhari	k-hah·ree	man
qhatuy	k-hah·tui	to sell at a market
qhatu	k-hah·too	market
qhawachiy	k-hah·wah·chee	to show
qhawariy	k-hah·wah·ree	to look • to look after
qhaway	k-hah·wai	to watch • to see • care
qhilli	k-he·lyee	dirty
qhipapi	k-he·pah·pee	behind
qhipata	k-he·pah·tah	afterwards
qhipay	k-he·pai	to stay • to remain
qhusi	k-ho·see	blue (of eyes only)

Q'

q'aytu	k'ai·too	string
q'ipi	k'e·pee	backpack • package
q'ipiy	k'e·pee	to carry (on the back)
q'iyachay	k'e·yah·chai	to become infected
q'uchukuy	k'o·choo·kui	to celebrate

q'uncha	k'on·chah	stove
q'uñi	k'o·nyee	warm • hot
q'uñikuy	k'o·nyee·kui	to warm up
q'uñiy	k'o·nyee	to heat
q'upa	k'o·pah	garbage • rubbish
q'usmi	k'os·mee	smoke
q'usñi	k'os·nyee	smoke
q'uturichiy	k'o·too·ree·chee	to entertain

R

rakiy	rah·kee	to separate
rantiy	rahn·tee	to buy • to exchange • to barter
raphi	rah·p-hee	sheet (paper)
rap'a	rah·p'ah	page
raqch'i	rahkh·ch'ee	ceramic • pottery
raqra kunka	rahkh·rah koon·kah	hoarse
ratuchalla	rah·too·chah·lyah	fast (time)
ratulla	rah·too·lyah	quickly
rawray unquy	row·rai on·koy	temperature • fever
-rayku	·rai·koo	reason • because of
raymi	rai·mee	festival • holiday
rikch'akuq	reekh·ch'ah·kokh	lookalike • similar
rikch'aq	reekh·ch'ahkh	kind (type)
rikch'arichiy	reekh·ch'ah·ree·chee	to wake
rikch'ariy	reekh·ch'ah·ree	to wake
riki	ree·kee	of course
rikuchikuy	ree·koo·chee·kui	gift • present
rikurichiy	ree·koo·ree·chee	to exhibit
rikuy	ree·kui	to see
riluh	ree·lookh	clock • watch
rimay	ree·mai	to speak • to talk • language • word
rimaykuy	ree·mai·kui	to explain
ripuy	ree·pui	to leave • to go away
riqsichiy	rekh·see·chee	to show • to introduce (a person)
riqsinakuqmasi	rekh·see·nah·kokh·mah·see	friend
riqsisqa	rekh·sees·kah	famous
riqsiy	rekh·see	to know (people/places) • to get to know • to recognise
riy	ree	to go
rumi	roo·mee	rock • stone
runa	roo·nah	humankind • people • person • Quechua speaker

QUECHUA – ENGLISH DICTIONARY

S

runakuna	roo·nah·*koo*·nah	people
rupha	roo·p-hah	fever • temperature • hot
ruphariy	roo·*p-hah*·ree	to feel hot (person)
ruphay	roo·p-hai	burn • sunlight
ruqya	rokh·yah	noise
ruq'tu	rokh'·too	deaf
ruruy	roo·rui	to produce
ruwana	roo·*wah*·nah	job
ruwanayuq	roo·wah·*nah*·yokh	busy
ruwasqa	roo·*wahs*·kah	done (a task)
ruway	roo·wai	to do • to make

S

saksasqa	sahkh·*sahs*·kah	full (after a meal)
saku	sah·koo	jacket (of a man)
samariy	sah·*mah*·ree	to breathe
samay	sah·mai	rest (relax) • to rest
sami	sah·mee	luck
samiyuq	sah·mee·yokh	lucky
sapa	sah·pah	alone • each • every
sapanka	sah·*pahn*·kah	each • every
sapaq	sah·pahkh	different • other
saqillay	sah·ke·lyai	to allow • to permit
saqiy	sah·kay	to leave something
saruy	sah·rui	to step on
sasa	sah·sah	hard • difficult
sat'iy	sah·t'ee	to inject • to puncture
sayachiy	sah·*yah*·chee	to stop (someone else)
sayaq	sah·yahkh	steep
sayarichiy	sah·yah·*ree*·chee	to build
sayay	sah·yai	to stop (oneself) • to stand • size • to size
sayk'usqa	sai·k'*oos*·kah	tired
saywa	sai·wah	border
sichus	see·choos	if
siki	see·kee	bottom (body)
silq'u	sel·k'o	signature
simi	see·mee	language • word • mouth • lip
sinchi	seen·chee	strong (person) • very
sipas	see·pahs	young woman
sipascha	see·*pahs*·chah	young woman
siq'inchay	se·k'en·chai	to draw
siqay	se·kai	to climb
siqsiy	sekh·see	itch (sensation)
siray	see·rai	to sew
sirikuy	see·*ree*·kui	to lie down

**D
I
C
T
I
O
N
A
R
Y**

T

siriy	see·ree	to lie down
sispa	sees·pah	near • close
siwk	syookh	smooth • straight
sulpáy niy	sool·*pai* nee	to thank
sumaq	soo·mahkh	handsome • beautiful • nice • tasty
sumaq kawsayniyuq	soo·mahkh kow·sai·*nee*·yokh	honest
suni	soo·nee	long (length) • high
sunqu tupachiy	son·ko too·*pah*·chee	to (be in) love
suphu	soo·p·hoo	hair (body or animal)
suti	soo·tee	name
suti silq'uy	soo·*tee* sel·k'oy	to sign (a document)
sutichay	soo·*tee*·chai	to call • to name
sut'u	soo·t'oo	wet
suwakuy	soo·*wah*·kui	to rob
suway	soo·wai	to steal
suwirti	soo·*weer*·tee	luck
suyay	soo·yai	to expect • to wait
suyk'u	sui·k'oo	cup
suynay	sui·nai	sound
suyt'u	sui·t'oo	long (length) • high
suyu	soo·yoo	region

T

-ta	·tah	towards • to
taki	*tah*·kee	song
takiy	*tah*·kee	to sing
taksa	*tahkh*·sah	short • average
taksa puñuna	*tahkh*·sah poo·*nyoo*·nah	twin bed
takuriy	tah·*koo*·ree	to disturb
tanqay	*tahn*·kai	to push
tanta	*tahn*·tah	crowd • group
tapuna	tah·*poo*·nah	question
tapunakuy	tah·poo·*nah*·kui	to argue
tapuy	*tah*·pui	to ask (a question)
taqruy	*tahkh*·roy	to mix
tarikuy	tah·*ree*·kui	to find (something lost)
tarpuy	*tahr*·pui	to plant
tawa k'uchuyuq	*tah*·wah k'oo·*choo*·yokh	square (shape)
tayriyay	tai·*ree*·yai	to be late
timpuraq	teem·*poo*·rahkh	early in the afternoon
tinku	*teen*·koo	average • medium-sized
tinkuy	*teen*·kui	to meet • to meet up with
tiqsimuyu	tekh·see·*moo*·yoo	world • universe • space • time • Earth

tiyana	tee·*yah*·nah	chair • seat
tiyay	tee·yai	to live in • to sit
trawu	trah·woo	alcohol • liquor
trukiy	troo·kee	to barter • to exchange
tukay	too·kai	to play (music)
tukuy	too·kui	to finish • end • limit • everything • every • all
tullpa	*tooly*·pah	clay stove
tullu	too·lyoo	bone • thin • skinny
tupay	too·pai	to meet • to meet up with
tura	too·rah	friend (male friend of woman)
turi	too·ree	brother (of woman)
turiyay	too·*ree*·yai	to make fun of
tusuy	too·sui	dance • to dance
tuta	too·tah	evening • night • dark
tuta mikhuy	too·tah *mee*·k-hui	dinner
tutallamanta	too·tah·lyah·*mahn*·tah	early in the morning
tutamanta mikhuna	too·tah·*mahn*·tah mee·*k*·hoo·nah	breakfast
tutaraq	too·*tah*·rahkh	early in the morning
tutayay	too·*tah*·yai	to get dark
tuwalla	too·*wah*·lyah	towel

TH

thanta	t-han·tah	old (worn out)
thatkiy	t-haht·kee	to step

T'

t'aqasqa	t'ah·*kahs*·kah	separated
t'aqay	t'ah·kai	to separate
t'aqsay	t'ahkh·sai	to wash (clothes/hair)
t'ikray	t'eekh·rai	to translate
t'uqu	t'o·ko	hole • window
t'uru	t'oo·roo	mud

U

uhay	oo·hai	drink • to drink
uhu	oo·hoo	cough
uhuy	oo·hui	to cough
ukhu	oo·k·hoo	deep • inside
ukhupi	oo·*k*·hoo·pee	inside • among
ukyay	ookh·yai	drink • to drink
uliyay	oo·*lee*·yai	baptism

uma llaqta	oo·mah lyahkh·tah	capital city
unay	oo·nai	delay • to delay • past
upa	oo·pah	mute • deaf
uran	oo·rahn	below
uray	oo·rai	under
urmay	oor·mai	to fall
urpi	oor·pee	dove (also an endearment)
urpu	oor·poo	jar
usa	oo·sah	lice
usqhaq	oos·k-hakh	speedy
usqhay	oos·k-hai	fast • quickly (movement)
usqhaypaq	oos·k-hai·pahkh	urgent
usqhayta	os·k-hai·tah	immediately • very soon
ususi	oo·soo·see	daughter (of father)
utaq	oo·tahkh	or
uyakuy	oo·yah·kui	to agree to • to accept
uyariy	oo·yah·ree	to hear • to listen • to understand

W

wahay	wah·hai	to call (shout/telephone)
wakcha	wahkh·chah	poor • poor person
wakcha kay	wahkh·chah kai	poverty
wakin	wah·keen	part • rest (remaining)
wakinkunalla	wah·keen·koo·nah·lyah	some (animate object)
wakiwakillan	wah·kee·wah·kee·lyan	some (inanimate object)
waksi	wahkh·see	steam
wampar	wahm·pahr	table
wampu	wahm·poo	boat
-wan	·wahn	with
wañusqa	wah·nyoos·kah	dead
wañuy	wah·nyui	to die
waq	wahkh	other
waqachiy	wah·kah·chee	to play (music)
waqay	wah·kai	to cry
waqaychay	wah·kai·chai	to keep
waqllichiy	wahkh·lyee·chee	to detour
waqlliy	wahkh·lyee	to detour
waqtanpi	wahkh·tahn·pee	beside (next to)
waqtu	wahkh·too	alcohol • liquor
waqyay	wahkh·yai	to call (shout/telephone)
waq'a	wah·k'ah	crazy
wara	wah·rah	underpants • trousers

warmi	*wahr*·mee	wife • woman
warmichakuy	wahr·mee·*chah*·kui	to marry (man says)
wasi	wah·see	house
wasi ayllu	wah·see *ai*·lyoo	home
wasi-masi	wah·see·*mah*·see	neighbour
waskha	wahs·k·hah	rope
wata	wah·tah	year • age
wata hunt'ay	wah·tah *hoon*·t'ai	birthday
watay	wah·tai	to tie
watiqmanta	wah·tekh·*mahn*·tah	again
watukuy	wah·*too*·kui	to miss (person) • to visit
waturikuy	wah·too·*ree*·kui	to visit
watuq	wah·tokh	fortune teller
wat'a	wah·t'ah	island
wawa	wah·wah	baby (human)
wawa qhawaq	wah·wah k·hah·wahkh	babysitter
wawtisay	wow·*tee*·sai	baptism
wayaqa	wah·*yah*·kah	bag • purse • handbag
wayk'uy	wai·k'ui	to cook
wayllunakuy	wai·lyoo·*nah*·kui	to fall in love
waylluy	wai·lyui	love • to love
waylluq	wai·lokh	lover
wayna	wai·nah	young man
wayqi	wai·ke	brother (of man) • friend (male friend of man)
wayq'u	wai·k'o	deep valley
wayra	wai·rah	air
wayt'ay	wai·t'ai	to swim
wichay	wee·chai	to climb • up • uphill • north
wiksayuq	weekh·*sah*·yokh	pregnant (human)
willa	wee·lyah	news
willachikuy	wee·lyah·*chee*·kui	message
willakuy	wee·*lyah*·kui	to confess (tell) • story
willay	wee·lyai	to advise • to inform • to warn
wintana	ween·*tah*·nah	window
wiñay	wee·nyai	to grow • age
wiñay hunt'asqa	wee·nyai hoon·t'*ahs*·kah	adult
wira	wee·rah	fat • grease
wisikilita	wee·see·kee·*lee*·tah	bicycle
wisq'ana	wees·k'*ah*·nah	lock
wisq'asqa	wees·k'*ahs*·kah	shut
wisq'ay	wees·k'ai	to close • to shut
wulsiku	wool·*see*·koo	pocket
wutilla	woo·*tee*·lyah	bottle
wutilla kichana	woo·*tee*·lyah kee·*chah*·nah	bottle opener

Y

yachachiy	yah·chah·chee	to teach • to explain
yachay	yah·chai	to learn • to know (facts) • education
yachayniyuq	yah·chai·nee·yokh	intelligent • wise
yananchakuy	yah·nahn·chah·kui	to marry • wedding
yanapay	yah·nah·pai	to aid • to assist • to help
yanqallan	yahn·kah·lyahn	free (no cost)
yapamanta	yah·pah·mahn·tah	again
yapa yapa	yah·pah yah·pah	often
yaqa	yah·kah	almost • more or less
yawarchay	yah·wahr·chai	to bleed
yaya	yah·yah	priest • God
yunka	yoon·kah	jungle • forest
yupay	yoo·pai	to count
yupaychay	yoo·pai·chai	to respect • to worship
yupaychay wasi	yoo·pai·chai wah·see	temple
yuray	yoo·rai	to plant
yuyay	yoo·yai	to think • to remember • thought
yuyay quy	yoo·yai koy	advice
yuyariy	yoo·yah·ree	to remember
yuyaychay	yoo·yai·chai	to advise • to counsel
yuyaysapa	yoo·yai·sah·pah	intelligent • wise
yuyayukuy	yoo·yah·yoo·kui	to realise

SUSTAINABLE TRAVEL

As the climate change debate heats up, the matter of sustainability becomes an important part of the travel vernacular. In practical terms, this means assessing our impact on the environment and local cultures and economies – and acting to make that impact as positive as possible. Here are some basic phrases to get you on your way …

COMMUNICATION & CULTURAL DIFFERENCES

I'd like to learn some of your local dialects.
nyoo·*kah*·kah *mai*·kahn
kahn·pahkh *lyahk*·tah
ree·mai·koo·*nah*·tah
yah·chah·hoo·*nah*·yahn

*Ñuqaqa maykan
qanpaq llakta
rimaykunata
yachajunayan.*

Would you like me to teach you some English?
ah·shah een·*glee*·stah nyoo·kah
yah·cha·chee·*chee*·nah *kahn*·tah
moo·nahn·*kee*·choo?

*¿Asha inglista ñuqa
yachachichina qanta
munankichu?*

Is this a local or national custom?
kai·kah *nyow*·pah kow·*sah*·nah
kai·mahn·*tah*·choo kai
mah·mah·lyahk·*tah*·choo kah·pahn?

*¿Kayqa ñawpa kawsana
kaymantachu kay
mamallaktachu kapan?*

COMMUNITY BENEFIT & INVOLVEMENT

What sorts of issues is this community facing?
kai ai·lyoo·koo·*nah*·kah ee·mah
lah·yah har·kah·koo·*nah*·tah
cheen·pah·*nah*·joon?

*¿Kay ayllukunaqa ima
laya jarkakunata
chinpanajun?*

media control	wee·lyai·koo·nah·*mahn*·tah *kah*·mai	*willaykuna-manta kamay*
political unrest	ah·poo kah·*mah*·yookh *mah*·nah kah·*see*·lyah *tee*·ahkh	*apu kamayuq mana kasilla tiaq*

poor living conditions	*wahk*·chah	waqcha
	kow·sai·*koo*·nah	kawsaykuna
religious conflict	pah·chah·kah·	pachaka-
	mahk·*mahn*·tah	makmanta
	mah·kah·*nah*·kui	makanakuy

I'd like to volunteer my skills.
    nyoo·kah yah·chah·nah·*koo*·nah   *Ñuqa yachanakuna*
    koo·*yah*·nah moo·nah·*yah*·nahn   *kuyana munayanan.*

Are there any volunteer programs available in the area?
    ee·mah mah·*kee*·tah koo·*yah*·nah   *¿Ima makita kuyana*
    yoo·yah·*nah*·kui *kahn*·pahkh   *yuyanakuy kanpaq*
    lyahk·*tah*·pee tee·*ahn*·choo?   *llaktapi tianchu?*

ENVIRONMENT

Where can I recycle this?
    mai·*pee*·tahkh *kai*·tah *koo*·teekh   *¿Maypitaq kayta kutiq*
    moo·*shook*·pee roo·rah·nah·*koo*·nee?   *mushuqpi ruranakuni?*

TRANSPORT

Can we get there by public transport?
    nyoo·kahn·*cheek*·kah   *¿Ñuqanchikqa*
    too·*kui*·pahkh ahn·tah·*wahn*·pee   *tukuypaq antawanpi*
    chai·mahn cha·yah·*nah*·tah   *chayman chayanata*
    oo·shah·neen·*cheek*·choo?   *ushaninchikchu?*

Can we get there by bicycle?
    nyoo·kahn·*cheek*·kah   *¿Ñuqanchikqa*
    peesh·kee·lee·*too*·pee   *pishkilitupi*
    chai·mahn cha·yah·*nah*·tah   *chayman chayanata*
    oo·shah·neen·*cheek*·choo?   *ushaninchikchu?*

I'd prefer to walk there.
    nyoo·*kah*·kah poo·ree·*ee*·mahn   *Ñuqaqa puriiman*
    chai·mahn   *chayman.*

ACCOMMODATION

I'd like to stay at a locally run hotel.

nyoo·*kah*·kah shookh kai	*Ñuqaqa shuq kay*
lyahk·tah *roo*·nah kah·*mah*·cheek	*llakta runa kamachik*
poo·*nyoo*·nah wah·*see*·pee	*puñuna wasipi*
poo·nyoo·*nah*·yahn	*puñunayan.*

Can I turn the air conditioning off and open the window?

wai·rah·*chee*·tah	*¿Wayrachita*
wah·nyoo·chee·*shah*·choo	*wañuchishachu*
kah·wah·nah·*tah*·peesh	*kawanatapish*
pahs·kahn·*gah*·pahkh	*paskangapaq*
oo·shah·*nee*·choo?	*ushanichu?*

Are there any ecolodges here?

kai lyahk·tah·*mahn*·tah	*¿Kay llaktamanta*
wah·*see*·pee poo·nyoon·*gah*·pahkh	*wasipi puñungapaq*
tee·ahn?	*tian?*

There's no need to change my sheets.

nyoo·kah pah·*chah*·tah *mah*·nah	*Ñuqa pachata mana*
moo·*dahn*·kee sah·*kee*·lyah	*mudanki sakilla.*

SHOPPING

Where can I buy locally produced souvenirs?

mai·*pee*·tahkh *ee*·mah	*¿Maypitaq ima*
mah·kee·roo·rahsh·*kah*·tah kai	*makirurashqata kay*
lyahk·*tah*·pee rahn·deen·*gah*·pahkh	*llaktapi randingapaq*
oo·*shah*·nee?	*ushani?*

Is this made from animal skins?

kai·kah *chee*·tah kah·rah·*koo*·nah	*¿Kayqa chita karakuna*
roo·*rahsh*·kah *kahn*·choo?	*rurashqa kanchu?*

Which forests are these products sourced from?

mai·hahn sah·chah·*mahn*·tah kai	*¿Mayjan sachamanta kay*
mah·kee·roo·*rahsh*·kah	*makirurashqa*
ah·pah·*moon*·kee?	*apamunki?*

FOOD

Do you sell …?	kahn·choo hah·too·*koon*·kee …?	¿Qanchu jatukunki …?
locally produced food	kai lyahk·*tah*·pee mee·*koo*·nah roo·rahsh·*kah*·tah	kay llaktapi mikuna rurashqata
organic produce	kai aly·*pah*·pee lyook·sheesh kah·*koo*·nah	kay allpapi llukshish qakuna

Can you tell me what traditional foods I should try?

kahn·kah oo·shan·*kee*·choo
mai·hahn kai·*mahn*·tah
mee·koo·nah·koo·*nah*·tah nyoo·kah
mah·lyeen·*gah*·pahkh moo·*nah*·nee?

¿Qanqa ushankichu mayjan kaymanta mikunakunata ñuqa mallingapaq munani?

SIGHTSEEING

Does your company …?	kahn·pahkh rahn·*dee*·nah·kah·*too*·nah …?	¿Qanpaq randinakatuna …?
donate money to charity	kooly·*kee*·tah kah·rai wahk·chah·koo·*nah*·tah kah·rah·*pai*·choo	kullkita karay waqchakunata karapaychu
hire local guides	kai lyahk·tah·*mahn*·tah poo·shahk·*koo*·nah meen·*gah*·gree	kay llaktamanta pushaqkuna mingagri
visit local businesses	ree·koo·green·*kee*·choo rahn·*dee*·nah·kah·*too*·nah wah·see·koo·*nah*·mahn kai lyahk·*tah*·pee	rikugrinkichu randinakatuna wasikunaman kay llaktapi

Are cultural tours available?

ree·cheek poo·reen·*gah*·pahkh
tee·*ahn*·choo?

¿Richik puringapaq tianchu?

don't just stand there, say something!

What kind of traveller are you?

A. You're eating chicken for dinner *again* because it's the only word you know.

B. When no one understands what you say, you step closer and shout louder.

C. When the barman doesn't understand your order, you point frantically at the beer.

D. You're surrounded by locals, swapping jokes, email addresses and experiences
  – other travellers want to borrow your phrasebook or audio guide.

If you answered A, B, or C, you NEED Lonely Planet's language products ...

- **Lonely Planet Phrasebooks** – for every phrase you need in every language
  you want
- **Lonely Planet Language & Culture** – get behind the scenes of English as it's
  spoken around the world – learn and laugh
- **Lonely Planet Fast Talk & Fast Talk Audio** – essential phrases for short trips and
  weekends away – read, listen and talk like a local
- **Lonely Planet Small Talk** – 10 essential languages for city breaks
- **Lonely Planet Real Talk** – downloadable language audio guides from
  lonelyplanet.com to your MP3 player

... and this is why

- **Talk to everyone everywhere**
  Over 120 languages, more than any other publisher
- **The right words at the right time**
  Quick-reference colour sections, two-way dictionary, easy pronunciation,
  every possible subject – and audio to support it

Lonely Planet Offices

Australia
90 Maribyrnong St, Footscray,
Victoria 3011
☎ 03 8379 8000
fax 03 8379 8111
✉ talk2us@lonelyplanet.com.au

USA
150 Linden St, Oakland,
CA 94607
☎ 510 250 6400
fax 510 893 8572
✉ info@lonelyplanet.com

UK
2nd floor, 186 City Rd
London EC1V 2NT
☎ 020 7106 2100
fax 020 7106 2101
✉ go@lonelyplanet.co.uk

lonelyplanet.com